Quirin Pinyin Updated Editions

(QPUE)

New editions that update and revise classics of Western sinology in line with current scholarship and practices (e.g. the older Wade-Giles transliteration of Chinese words updated to the current Pinyin standard).

Series titles include the following *Revised Editions*:

The Poetry of the Early Tang, by Stephen Owen

The Great Age of Chinese Poetry: The High Tang, by Stephen Owen

Taoism and Chinese Religion, by Henri Maspero

Zen Dust: The History of the Koan and Koan Study in Rinzai (Linji) Zen, by Isshu Miura and Ruth Fuller Sasaki

Lunheng: The Complete Essays of Wang Chong, Translated & annotated by Alfred Forke

Yin-Yang
and the Nature of
Correlative Thinking

A. C. Graham

Revised Edition

QUIRIN PRESS
Melbourne & Basel
2016

Published by Quirin Press
P.O. Box 4226, Melbourne University, Vic. 3052, Australia
E-mail: enquiries@quirinpress.com
http://www.quirinpress.com

Copyright © 1986 by A. C. Graham
Copyright © 2016 by Quirin Press for this second revised edition.

All rights reserved. No part of this publication may be reproduced or transmitted in any form or by any means, electronic or mechanical, including photocopying, recording or otherwise stored in a retrieval system, without prior permission in writing from the publishers.

The National Library of Australia Cataloging-in-Publication entry:
    Graham, A. C. (Angus Charles), 1919–1991, author.
    Yin-Yang and the Nature of Correlative Thinking
    Revised edition.
    ISBN: 9781922169181 (paperback)
    Quirin Pinyin Updated Editions (QPUE)
    Includes bibliographical references and index.
    Cosmology, Chinese | Philosophy, Chinese | Yin-yang
    Graham, A. C. (Angus Charles), 1919–1991, author
    181.11
    ISBN: 978-1-922169-18-1 (pbk.)
    ISBN: 978-1-922169-19-8 (E-book)

∞ Printed on acid-free paper

CONTENTS

Publisher's Note — viii

1. Introduction — 1
2. The principles of a structuralist approach — 29
3. Pairs: the Yin and Yang — 45
4. Fours and fives: the Five Phases — 75
5. Binary structure: the *Changes* — 121

Appendix: The early history of Yin-Yang and the Five Phases. — 129

Finding list — 167
Notes — 171
Index — 181

Publisher's Note to the Quirin Press Revised Edition

The present publication in the Quirin Pinyin Updated Editions (QPUE) series updates and revises *Yin-Yang and the Nature of Correlative Thinking*, by A. C. Graham, which was originally published by The Institute of East Asian Philosophies, Singapore, in 1986.

The revisions bring this title in line with current scholarship and practices. Apart from updating the older Wade-Giles transliteration of Chinese words to the current *pinyin* standard, the text has been fully re-set and any inconsistencies and typographical errors corrected.

For the sake of consistency, Chinese names in bibliographic entries have been updated to *pinyin*, even though any Wade-Giles transliterations in English language titles have been retained. An index has been added, including Chinese characters where appropriate. Chinese characters have also been added to the text where appropriate, save for any characters that could not be established from original sources with absolute certainty.

For the parts they have played in the production and publication of this revised edition of A. C. Graham's unique work, we are indebted to a number of people and organisations. Our thanks go to the author's widow Mrs. Der Bao (Judy) Graham for permission to re-issue this title; and to Cheryl Hutty for proofing the work and implementing the extensive *pinyin* updating and checking of all the Chinese characters.

Quirin Press
Melbourne, 2016

1
INTRODUCTION

Cosmological speculation, which is at the beginnings of Greek philosophy, entered the main current of Chinese thought only at the very end of the classical period. It is possible to spend a long time studying the philosophers from Confucius (551–479 BCE) to Han Fei 韓非 (died 233 BCE) without ever having to come to terms with it. One more step, however, into the *Lüshi chunqiu* 呂氏春秋 (c. 240 BCE) and the appendices to the *Changes*, and one must find an entry into a vast system relating community to cosmos in an order which juxtaposes the harmonious and separates the conflicting, starting from chains of pairs with contrasting members correlated with the Yin and Yang, branching out into fours and fives (Four Seasons, Four Directions, Five Colours, Five Sounds, Five Tastes, Five Smells …) correlated with the Five Phases, and down through successive divisions correlated with the Eight Trigrams and Sixty-four Hexagrams. This scheme, in which to explain or infer is to fill a place in the pattern, provides the organising concepts of proto-sciences such as astronomy, medicine, music, divination, and in later centuries alchemy and geomancy. The correlative thinking of China, to which Marcel Granet's *La pensée chinoise* (1934) remains an unsurpassed introduction, is not wholly strange to a Westerner who remembers the Four Elements, Four Humours and Pythagorean numerology in the past of his own tradition, but during the last few centuries this style of system-building has become so remote to most of us that access is now difficult except for people temperamentally in sympathy with the one Western study in which it still flourishes, occultism. The present paper will combine inquiries into Chinese cosmology and into the nature of correlative thinking in general, with a great deal of freewheeling backwards and forwards, in the hope that they will cast light on each other.

There is nothing obsolete or foreign about correlative thinking as such; it is going on all the time in the background of every other kind of thought. The great interest of system-building of the Yin-Yang type, odd as its results may seem, is that it tries to lay out explicitly the full range of comparisons and contrasts which other kinds of thinking leave implicit. Simply to apply a common name one has already to be classing as similar and distinguishing from the dissimilar. Even at the pre-linguistic level of perception, to fill a gap in a figure and perceive it as a *Gestalt* implies correlation of similarities and differences, although as a simultaneous act which does not distinguish part from whole. Inference by analogy assumes a system of similarities and differences within which the analogue counts as similar, but the system remains implicit. Analytic thinking assumes the assimilations and differentiations embodied in the vocabulary of the language, but only in emergency reverses its direction to examine and criticise them. We do find correlation of the building-blocks of thought, of the same kind as in the most exotic of cosmologies, in the acquisition of language itself, which may indeed be claimed as the one activity to which correlative thinking is *perfectly* adequate. Having become familiar with the oppositions "cat/cats," "shoe/shoes," "stone/stones" one immediately fills the gap in "house/–" with "houses"; and if one slips into the error "goose/gooses" and is corrected, one automatically correlates "goose/geese" with "foot/feet," "tooth/teeth." In learning to speak grammatically, it is analytic thinking which is inadequate, useful as it is a preliminary tool; a foreign language is fully mastered only when one is no longer deliberately applying a memorised rule distinguishing singular from plural. Nevertheless, even in language, correlative thinking is a subterranean process which becomes conscious only intermittently; it is only when doubt arises that one asks, "Should I say it like this or like that?" Similarly it is only when in difficulties that a philosopher begins to question the correlations of concepts in the background of his own thought. Although mediaeval and Renaissance cosmologies may well expose underlying assimilations and differentiations as clearly as the Chinese, the latter have a special advantage for our purposes. An effect of the tendency to parallelism so prominent in Classical Chinese style is that the play of comparison and contrast which we dimly perceive at the bottom of our own thought seems closer to the surface in China. One has the impression that Chinese culture, at least on its Taoist side, enjoys a much easier recognition and more comfortable acceptance of the looseness of fit between concept and object. Thus *Laozi* is already undermining conventional assumptions by reversing the priorities in the standard oppositions "high/low," "strong/weak," "male/female," in a manner suggestive of the reversals which are the post-structuralist Jacques Derrida's initial move in the brand-new enterprise of deconstructing the conceptual scheme of the West.

In Granet's time it was still natural to assume that in matters of fact, as in geometry, demonstration can start from clearly defined terms independent of correlations, so that Yin-Yang thinking – not that he treats it unsympathetically – belongs to a stage which Greek logic put behind it once and for all. By now, however, it has come to seem that wherever you dig down towards the roots of analytic reason, you reach a stratum where thinking is correlative, so that it becomes necessary to look at Yin-Yang from another direction. We may take examples from two widely influential books of the last half century, Gilbert Ryle's *Concept of mind* and Thomas Kuhn's *Structure of scientific revolutions*, restating their positions in the terminology which we shall be using, that of correlative ratios. Ryle sets out to discredit the dichotomy of a body which is extended in space and a mind which is not. He points out that to assume that mind is different in kind from, yet interacts with, the body which is a machine, implies crediting it with a similarity, that its activities like the body's have causes and effects. The mind as "ghost in a machine" has to be conceived as "a spectral machine." This leads to well-known difficulties; how can willing, which is non-spatial, cause the limbs to move in space, or the mind's perception of a colour be the effect of a process in the optic nerve? Ryle sees the problem as arising from an improper correlation in the metaphorising at the back of thought, "Mind : head, hands, feet :: ruler : subjects" (the "para-political myth"), which the advent of mechanistic science turned into "Mind : head, hands, feet :: governor engine : other engines" (the "para-mechanical myth"). He invites us instead to try out new correlations, "Mind : head, hands, feet :: University : colleges, libraries, playing fields," or "Mind : head, hands, feet :: the British constitution : Parliament, judiciary, Church of England." On this approach, the correlations deposited by habit or initiated by new insights are prior to the possibility of logical demonstration; one digs down to them and analyses their similarities and differences, then judges which to prefer by whether the arguments which start from them lead into or avoid logical difficulties. Kuhn has a similar approach to philosophy of science. He holds that a scientist's operations cannot be reduced to the application of formulated concepts, rules and laws, since he comes to understand these only in the course of learning to apply them in practice; he acquires his skill in handling them by correlating with concrete exemplars of problem-solving, "Doing this : this problem :: doing that : that problem." The work of a scientific community assumes, behind all its formulated laws of nature, a shared "paradigm," its own specific constellation of beliefs, values and techniques, centred on the concrete exemplars which are paradigms in the narrow sense. Science for Kuhn, like philosophy of mind for Ryle, starts from correlations which it can neither validate nor escape, without however being imprisoned by any one or other of them; there are "scientific revolutions" at which the accumulation of unsolved problems within the old paradigm leads to crisis, a correlative switch and a new paradigm more adequate to solving them.

The problems faced by Ryle and Kuhn are ones which every serious inquirer into Chinese philosophy is driven by his own experience to discover for himself. At first he is likely to assume that his business is to detach Chinese ideas from the metaphors which disguise them, and re-root them in his own self-evident concepts. But he cannot ask such a question as "Does Chinese science recognise laws of nature?" without noticing that his own concept of law is likewise rooted in metaphor. It may then perhaps occur to him that when he ponders the question of free will, his abstract knowledge that the statistical regularities of science differ in many respects from acts of Parliament does not stop him thinking as though "Laws of nature : nature :: man's laws : man"; he is still assuming that if even his willed actions "obey," "are subject to," "are bound by" the laws of nature, he is unfree as he would be if unable to disobey human laws. Recognition that Western and Chinese thought depend equally on correlations beyond the reach of logical demonstration seem to plunge him into relativism, and with the further recognition that analysis never attains its ideal of full mutual translatability, into cultural solipsism. Yet this scepticism conflicts with our experience that we do up to a point succeed in understanding Confucius or Laozi, by a co-ordination of concepts beyond the range of the translatable leading to Gadamer's "fusion of horizons." Here we are again forced to acknowledge that the operation of language itself is an activity in which analysis never quite catches up with correlation. Language as communication starts from a correlation of viewpoints, seen at its simplest in the exchanging of personal and demonstrative pronouns; the child soon learns that "your 'I' : my 'you' :: your 'you' : my 'I'" without having to analyse and infer that the pronouns have the same reference. We have mastered a foreign language when we cease to depend on the imperfect translations inside our heads, and simply speak it, leaving all translation behind; and in studying Chinese thought our understanding of a word in context is always a little ahead of our analyses of the differences from comparable terms in

Western philosophy. We cannot isolate ourselves in the realm of the fully analysed and imperfectly translatable without the threat of a solipsism which is not even coherent, since there are no clear boundaries separating the viewpoints of cultures, languages, even selves; a single person successfully correlates the idioms of his different social roles without ever having to translate from one into another.

Even in Western philosophy the correlative is not always a buried layer to be uncovered, there are fields where it still obstinately refuses to be trodden under. We may instance the prolonged efforts of moral philosophers to detach the Golden Rule ("Do to others as you would have them do to you") from correlative thinking and reformulate it as Kant's Categorical Imperative or as some more modern principle of universalisation. The Golden Rule prescribes that I put myself imaginatively in your place and correlate "I want A : do B for me :: you want C : ……," the gap filling with the spontaneous emergence of "Do D for you." But since it is the duty of a philosopher not to remain content with the unanalysed insights of common life, he must try to detach the rule from the correlating act and deduce "Do D for you" by combining it with propositions about the circumstances. For this the Golden Rule in its naive form is adequate only in the simplest case, where A, B, C and D are all equivalent. Pondering cases where A differs from C, or (what I want being bad for me) B from A, he finds himself drawn into an unending stream of reformulations and qualifications. The Golden Rule, which applied correlatively has been guiding moral discourse since Confucius, Gautama and Jesus, becomes for the analytic mind a principle so muddled that it becomes a mystery how it can ever have been usable.

A point which has become increasingly apparent in the 50 years since Granet's classic study is that whether in China or in the West to resort to correlative thinking in cosmology and the organisation of the proto-sciences has nothing whatever to do with the level of sophistication of thought in general. In the West the logic accepted as complete until the 19th century goes back to Aristotle, yet correlative thinking in the sciences prevailed right up to the Scientific Revolution about 1600. If we ask why Western thought was for 2,000 years "modern" in one field and "primitive" in the other, there is an obvious answer; the solution of logical problems requires no resources outside one's own head, of scientific a vast quantity of discrete information which, until some alternative approach is found, can be organised and utilised only by classifying as similar or different and inferring from similarities. Nor is cosmological correlation simply a method which has to be chosen in the absence of a viable alternative; even in its most luxuriant elaborations it is the refining of a cosmos in which the thinker already finds himself before his analytic thinking begins. I have only to discern that, for example, the sun and the king are alike in being "above" in power and glory, in the proportional opposition "sun : world :: king : men," to find myself already in a cosmos in which both have intelligible places, so that I can infer from their similarity both what to expect and how to respond; I must bow down in awe to the king as to the sun, grateful for his beneficence and reconciled to the incomprehensible caprices of unquestionable power. Nor should one suppose that reliance on correlative thinking in cosmos-building implies any failure to appreciate the value of causal explanation. It may be safely assumed that technology has from the first depended on causal thinking, on discoveries that when you do X the consequence is generally Y. It is a familiar observation that even in pre-literate cultures people do not resort to magic in fields such as the crafts which they understand causally. But piecemeal causal explanations do not add up to a cosmos, or even to a single organised science. Both in China and in the ancient and mediaeval West one meets a great deal of causal explanation and scepticism of the excesses of correlative cosmos-building, indeed whole episodes in which modern science seems in retrospect just around the corner, yet hardly a glimpse of the possibility of building a cosmos in any other way; criticism of cosmologists is not for correlative thinking as such, but for taking it to fantastic extremes beyond the limits of experience. Could it have been otherwise? Even a modern scientist is thinking correlatively (and at a level higher than the Kuhnian paradigm) as long as, for example, glimpses of patterns in the properties of the elements have not yet brought him in sight of a law of periodicity; until the drawing of a clear line between the testing of the law (which belongs to science) and the creative thinking behind it (which belongs to the scientist's biography), there would be no prospect of rejecting correlative systems as unscientific in principle.

The possibility of leaving proto-science behind resulted not from a gradual shift from correlative to causal explanation but from the quite sudden "Discovery of how to discover" about 1600. Until the West grasped the complicated idea of formulating mathematised laws of nature and testing them by controlled experiment, temporary swings in favour of causal explanation brought it no nearer to post-Galilean science. In the 15th and 16th centuries indeed the swing had been in the opposite direction. The Renaissance, tiring of Aristotelian common sense, revived

Pythagorean numerology, and revelling in its fantasies opened the way to the mathematisation of laws of nature. Inspired by Hermes Trismegistus and the Kabbalah, it conceived the prospect of conquering nature through magic before possessing the scientific means to realise it. (Prospero and Faustus are almost realistic pictures of the pioneers on the course which has led us to atom-splitting and space-travel). On the very threshold of modern science Kepler, whose three laws of planetary motion are the first true laws of nature since the Greeks, was trying to fit them into the symmetries of a cosmos in which sun, stars and planets correlate with the persons of the Trinity. Even after Galileo, correlative system-building remains invulnerable in any field not yet conquered by the new physics. Newton himself could without incongruity busy himself with alchemy and with correlating historical events with the predictions of the Apocalypse. One might put it this way: while thinking causally, attention is diverted from the correlating of concepts in the background; whenever there is nothing to put in front, correlative thinking is necessarily in the foreground. In the conduct of ordinary affairs, whenever circumstances are too complex and move too fast for analysis, there is likewise nothing in front of the instantaneous act of assimilation and differentiation.

Granet took it for granted that the mode of cosmological thinking in China was the mode of all thinking, in philosophy of the classical age as much as in alchemy and geomancy. How could Confucius and Mencius, Mozi, and Zhuangzi fail to exemplify what is by definition *la pensée chinoise*? A result of the research of the last 50 years which would have astonished Granet is that throughout the classical period correlative schematising belongs only to astronomers, diviners, musicmasters, physicians; the philosophers from Confucius to Han Fei do not engage in it at all. We find different levels of thinking in philosophy and in the proto-sciences very much as in Europe. Granted that there is less of analytic and more of analogical thinking among Chinese than among Greek philosophers, the abstention from schematising correspondences is if anything greater in China. This aspect of classical philosophy was for a long time obscured by the presence among the Confucian classics of the *Book of Changes*, the early Zhou manual of divination with appendices ascribed to Confucius, who himself once mentions the book with reverence in the standard text of the *Analects*. There, however, the reading *yi* 易 "Changes" is questionable since there is a variant *yi* 亦 "also, after all."[1] The first extant Confucian who unquestionably uses the *Changes* is Xunzi in the 3rd century BCE, not however as a classic; when naming in sequence the other five classics he leaves the *Changes* out.[2] The Yin and Yang are fully established in the philosophical literature as the two fundamental principles by about 300 BCE, but without yet being fitted into correlative schemes. As for the Five Phases, both the Mohist *Canons* and the military classic *Sunzi* declare flatly that 'The Five Phases have no regular conquests' (五行毋（＝無）常勝), and Han Fei mentions them only among methods of divination which he is deriding.[3] Xunzi's description of

Mencius and Zisi 子思 as teaching the *wu xing* 五行 is now known, from the Confucian document attached to Mawangdui manuscript A of *Laozi*,[4] to refer not to the Five Phases but to five kinds of conduct, benevolence, right, manners, wisdom and sagehood. Even among military texts which appeal to the conquest order of the Five Phases, none is confidently datable before the late 3rd century BCE.[5]

Unlike the philosophers, rulers and statesmen were, from as far back as we have records, very interested in natural phenomena, not of course from scientific curiosity, but as presages of good and ill fortune to the state. The historical narratives of the *Zuozhuan* 左傳 (4th century BCE) and the cognate *Guoyu* 國語 are full of such inquiries, answered in detail by physicians, historiographers, musicmasters and knowledgeable statesmen. The answers display great erudition in the proto-sciences, with Yin and Yang, Five Phases, schemes of colours, sounds, smells and tastes, and divination by the hexagrams of the *Changes*. The philosophers, however, keep aloof from all this, following the precedent set by

Confucius himself (*Analects* 7/2 子不語怪力亂神 'The Master did not speak of wonders, feats of strength, disturbances, the daemonic'). Not that they deny that it has its place in the conduct of ritual and government. Xunzi, while mentioning as an obvious fact that divination tells you nothing about the future, takes it for granted that it is a ritual obligation.[6] The military chapters of *Mozi*, from late in the 3rd century BCE, contain a fascinating description of the divinatory rite in preparation for attack by the enemy, with the standard correlations of cardinal points, numbers and colours.[7] We could hardly have guessed from the rest of the book that the Mohists did anything of the kind. In the only other passage which mentions these correlations Mozi is warned by a diviner not to travel north because his colour is black and 'Today God is killing the black dragon in the north' (帝以今日殺黑龍於北方); when he fails to get through and the diviner says, "I told you so," he replies that the white failed too, and that to listen to such advice would bring all travel to a stop.[8]

The one philosophical document earlier

than the *Lüshi chunqiu* which discusses scientific questions is the Mohist *Canons*. But here we find not appeal to Yin and Yang, the Five Phases and the hexagrams but strictly causal explanations applied only to optics and mechanics. Moreover, the practice has a principle behind it; conjunctions of events may be "necessary" (*bi* 必) or "appropriate" (*yi* 宜), conjunction with a cause (*gu* 故) is "necessary" but the conquest of metal by fire in the cycle of the Five Phases is merely "appropriate," the outcome depending on the quantities of fuel and of metal.[9] The *Canons* not only recognise the superiority of causal over correlative explanation but exclude the latter from the art of "dialectic" (*bian* 辯). Here we have what is perhaps the most striking Chinese parallel to those pre-modern Western swings towards causal explanation which do not lead to the "Discovery of how to discover." The Mohists offer only piecemeal explanations in terms of interference with the light or the vertical descent of weights, with no mathematics and no laws of nature. In traditional proto-sciences such as medicine they presumably had to be content with the appropriate as second best to the necessary. A possible exception would be astronomy, for which we have a document of unknown date, appended at the end of ch. 3 of *Huainanzi*, which makes an equally sharp break with the methods of Chinese proto-science.[10] Instead of arriving at the dimensions of Heaven and Earth through numerological symmetries, it explains how to calculate them from measurements of the sun's shadow by the gnomon, with illustrations using hypothetical numbers (the first number is introduced by the contra-factual *jia shi* 假使 "Supposing that…," and re-used in a later illustration). This approximation to what we would nowadays approve as true science is of course quite unusual, resulting from an interest in logical clarification and also in the crafts (notably military engineering) which was almost limited to the Later Mohist school; but in philosophical literature before 240 BCE it is the only kind of science we find.

When Sima Tan 司馬談 (died 110 BCE) retrospectively classified the pre-Han thinkers in Six Schools (*liu jia* 六家), he included a "School of Yin and Yang." Its founder Zou Yan 鄒衍 (c. 250 BCE), a man of Qi 齊 who won patronage in Yan 燕,[11] is therefore generally accepted as one of the major philosophers of the classical age. But one of the few things which may be said with confidence about Zou Yan is that he belongs to a world right outside the philosophical schools.[12] He is not even execrated or derided by them like the "egoist" Yang Zhu 揚朱 or the sophist Gongsun Long 公孫龍, he is totally ignored, even in the sources which list leaders of rival schools (*Xunzi*, *Lüshi chunqiu*, *Shizi* 尸子, the *Tianxia* 天下 chapter of *Zhuangzi*, *Huainanzi*).[13] The one pre-Han mention of him is in Han Fei's attack on divination, in connection not with his thought but, obscurely, with a defeat of Yan in 242 BCE in spite of favourable auspices.[14] Zou Yan belongs to the same world as the court historiographers and physicians of the *Zuozhuan*, but as a newcomer winning the ear of princes by the promise of esoteric knowledge; his followers in the states of Qi and Yan in the far North-East are the first to be remembered as *fangshi* 方士 "men of secret arts."

Like the cosmology documented in the *Zuozhuan*, Zou Yan's is known to us almost exclusively through a historical source, the *Shiji* 史記 of Sima Qian 司馬遷 (145–c. 90 BCE). Sima Qian pays attention to him because of the influence of his doctrines on the King of Qin 秦, who as First Emperor re-unified China in 221 BCE. Adopting Zou Yan's correlations of the rise and fall of dynasties with the conquest cycle of the Five Phases, the Qin Emperor selected the colour black and the number six to demonstrate that he reigned by the power of Water; and it was Zou Yan whom the *fangshi* from the North-East who promised the Emperor the secret of immortality claimed as their authority. Sima Qian himself contrasts the honours accorded Zou Yan by princes with their indifference to such better men as Confucius and Mencius.[15]

The eclectic *Lüshi chunqiu*, written in Qin about 240 BCE under the King who became First Emperor, is the earliest firmly dated philosophical text to lay out schemes of correspondences (although there are calendrical schemes in *Guanzi* 管子 which are likely to be a little earlier).[16] It includes correlations of the Five Phases both with the rise and fall of dynasties and with the royal calendar,[17] but it does not name Zou Yan. A little later, with reunification, the persecution of the schools, ascendancy of the *fangshi*, suppression of the classics but acceptance of the *Changes* as a manual of divination, the situation of the philosophers changed radically. The schools which revived with the victory of the Han in 202 BCE quickly adapted themselves to the now politically indispensable cosmology; the Confucian appendices to the *Changes* come at latest from very early in the Han. However, Zou Yan remained for the philosophers the outsider he had always been. Confucians no doubt borrowed directly or indirectly from his cosmology to compete with the *fangshi*, but as the sage of the *fangshi* themselves he could never be acknowledged. Han writers who discuss Zou Yan, notably Sima Qian, Huan Kuan 桓寬 and Wang Chong 王充, all treat him as a fantast, although Sima Qian does recognise that his thought has a moral dimension which he respects and that the *fangshi* did not fully understand him. The voluminous writings entered in the Han bibliography (Zouzi 鄒子, 49 *pian*: *Zouzi zhongshi* 鄒子終始 56 *pian*) seem to have been little read. Huan Kuan and Wang Chong write as though they know of his thought only through Sima Qian's biography.[18] The fragments which survive by quotation are negligible compared even, for example, with the remains of almost unheard-of minor Mohists appended to Sun Yirang's 孫詒讓 edition of *Mozi*.[19]

The Han dynasty is the time of the first flowering of Confucian and Taoist cosmology and of the first critic of its extravagances, the sceptic Wang Chong (CE 27–c. 100). By what criteria did traditional Chinese thinkers decide that correlative speculation is *going too far*? (For reasons already considered, they could not reject it in principle). In general this is a complicated question, but in the case of Zou Yan there is a straightforward answer. No one denied that we live on a square earth divisible into nine square parts (at the centre and in the cardinal and intermediate directions), but Zou Yan made himself notorious by declaring that this world is itself only one of nine continents separated by impassable seas, the features of which may be inferred by analogy with ours. For Sima Qian the purpose of a cosmic scheme is to organise information about the known world; his credulity lapses when Zou Yan extends the pattern and fills the gap with unseen lands and unremembered times.

Shiji (ch. 74) 2344
其語閎大不經，必先驗小物，推而大之，至於無垠。先序今以上至黃帝，學者所共術，大並世盛衰，因載其禨祥度制，推而遠之，至天地未生，窈冥不可考而原也。先列中國名山　大川，通谷禽獸，水土所殖，物類所珍，因而推之，及海外，人之所不能睹。

'His claims were extravagant and eccentric, he would always start the investigation from a smaller thing and infer to the larger, until he arrived at the boundless. He started by tracing from the present back to the Yellow Emperor, a tradition about which scholars agree, and having summed up the rises and declines of dynasties recorded their portents and institutions; then he inferred to the more remote, back to before Heaven and Earth were born, to the obscurity which cannot be fathomed by inquiry. He first listed China's famous mountains, great rivers, extensive valleys, birds and animals, the produce of the water and soil, the most precious kinds of things; then he inferred to what lies beyond the seas, to places which men are unable to observe.'

With the inclusion of the *Changes* among the Classics, Chinese thinkers could never again wholly ignore cosmology. We shall not pursue the later history of Chinese philosophy, but will risk the generalisation that it was fully committed to correlative thinking only during the Han, and that in its great periods (Neo-Taoism, Neo-Confucianism) systems of correspondences are always marginal to it rather than central.

2
THE PRINCIPLES OF A STRUCTURALIST APPROACH

If as we suggested there is a perfect fit between correlative thinking and the functioning of language itself, the most direct access should be by the structuralist approach inspired, by Saussure's linguistics. It seems advisable to explain at some length how we shall be using the two pairs of structuralist concepts especially useful for present purposes, "paradigm/syntagm" and "metaphor/metonym."

We start from the truisms that thinking is conducted in sentences composed of words drawn from the vocabulary of one's language, and that the words are already grouping in the "language" (*langue*) before entering the sentences of "speech" (*parole*). A sentence is formed, on the one hand by selecting words, on the other by combining them: the words relate "paradigmatically" as members of pairs or larger sets, "syntagmatically" as elements of the sentence.

	A	B	Paradigm
1.	He	They	
2.	posted	collected	
3.	a	the	
4.	letter.	mail.	

Syntagm

Verbal thinking draws on a stock of paradigms already grouping syntagmatically in chains of oppositions which at their simplest are binary:

	A	B	Paradigm
1.	Day	Night	
2.	Sun	Moon	
3.	Light	Darkness	
4.	Knowledge	Ignorance	
5.	Good	Evil	

Syntagm

(Here we number for convenience without implying succession or completeness).

On the syntagmatic plane the words already combine in English vocabulary or cliché in "daylight," "sunlight," "the light of knowledge," "the darkness of ignorance/of evil." But that we also say "moonlight" is a reminder that any chain interlocks with other chains, in the beginnings of a system. The moon is indeed darker, or at any rate dimmer, than the sun, but as itself luminous it enters into independent or subsidiary chains; we might for example have proceeded from Position 2 to

	A	B	Paradigm
3.	Sunlight	Moonlight	
4.	Constant	Fickle	
5.	Original	Copy	
6.	True	Deceitful	

Syntagm

This would lead us back again in the direction of "Good/evil." Here, however, the syntagmatic connections are more elusive, not congealed in the established formulae of the language.

These chains function as proportional oppositions: day is to night as good is to evil, day is to knowledge as night is to ignorance. Consequently, before we begin to think analytically in sentences we may already be said to "think," in the broad sense that we are already patterning experience and expecting the filling of gaps in the pattern. When the pattern is familiar this is no more than recurrence of the expectation, when a new pattern takes shape it is sudden insight, whether as the everyday intuitions of common sense or as the illuminations of the visionary and the fantast. The modern scientist, although his discoveries may start from such insights, does not trust them until confirmed by analysis; his objection to the correlative thinking of the pre-modern proto-sciences, whether Chinese or Western, is that it remains satisfied with the illusory self-evidence of what is *seen* to fit the pattern.

The system of interlocking chains emerges from and is initially confirmed by experience. The sun does regularly rise by day and the moon by night, the night does indeed bring ignorance of one's surroundings and dangers and evils. Since the choice of oppositions is guided by desire and aversion, which enchain with good and evil or superior and inferior, within the range of the system one knows not only what to expect but what to approve or disapprove. One has the prospect of a fully integrated cosmos such as China based on the Yin and Yang and the Five Phases, in which values are self-evident and one need think analytically only in order to pursue what immediately presents itself as good. But such a cosmos in taking shape expands beyond the bounds of what experience has verified. A Northern European may find himself continuing the original chain towards

	A	B	Paradigm
6.	White race	Black face	
7.	Blondes	Brunettes	

Syntagm

But he may notice that to assume black people to be savages, blonde girls sweet and innocent, and the *femme fatale* a brunette (with the brilliance and inconstancy of the moon added to the darkness and danger of night) sometimes clashes with observation.

He is then forced to analyse the syntagmatic relations critically, and give weight to the recurrent, and so causal, connection. A tension continues between the pressure of fact and the need for the security of remaining inside a fully comprehensible world. Causal relations begin to interlock, opening the prospect of another cosmos, that of modern science (which, on the argument we are pursuing, will be *inside* the adjusted, pruned down and submerged remainder of the older cosmos still implicit in the conceptual scheme of one's culture). Our position, however, is that there never was a serious prospect that piecemeal causal explanations would interrelate in a completed order until the "Discovery of how to discover" about 1600, when the West suddenly stumbled as though by accident on the winning combination of mathematised laws of nature with testing by controlled experiment. Up to 1600, the choice was between the cosmos of correlative thinking and no cosmos at all. That all schools of Chinese philosophy of the classical period refrained from pushing correlative thinking beyond the limits of verified experience by no means released them from this choice. They had to remain content with the barest outline of a cosmos, not much more than Heaven and Earth (or, at the very end of the period, the Yin and Yang) generating and destroying the 10,000 things through the cycles of the Four Seasons. There is the further point of course that even after the Scientific Revolution there remains a strong resistance to abandoning the cosmos which included oneself for one which has room only for an objectification of oneself, a cosmos in which prediction is more accurate than ever before but there is nothing which prescribes how to act.

Within the proportional oppositions, relations are of two kinds. Roman Jakobson describes paradigmatic relations as of "similarity/contrast," syntagmatic as of "contiguity/remoteness" (the latter understood to include the relation of part to whole).[20] Since Jakobson's "contiguity" covers all senses in which words or things may be described as "together," it may be more useful for present purposes to treat the syntagmatic as the plane of "connection/isolation." Proportional oppositions thus divide into

> A1 : B1 :: A2 : B2
> (Day compares with night as sun with moon)
> A1 : A2 :: B1 : B2
> (Day connects with sun as night with moon).

It will be noticed that although contrast on the paradigmatic plane implies similarity on the syntagmatic, it is a similarity between connections. "Milk : snow :: beer : mud," treated as a pure similarity/difference ratio for colour, liquidity, potability, would not enter a chain. It might do so, however, in a culture where the pure in heart drink milk, and dirt and squalor are expected to accompany beer, so that connections emerge between "milk/beer" and "snow/mud" which could enchain them with "light/darkness," "clean/dirty." A chain is not altogether self-generating even when it leads to such a ratio as "white man : black man :: good : evil"; there will be observed connections of racial differences with clashes of interest and divergent norms of conduct, the chain being extended to interpret them.

When relations tend to similarity rather than contrast, connection rather than isolation, one of a pair may substitute for the other by the figures of speech called "metaphor" and "metonymy."

	A	B	Paradigm	A	B
1.	King	Lion		King	Chairman
2.	Men	Beasts		Throne	Chair
Syntagm					

King is similar to lion as men to beasts, so by metaphor the lion is the king of the beasts and the king a lion among men. King connects with throne as chairman with chair, so by metonymy the monarchy is called the throne and the chairmanship the chair. (Since connection is assumed to include the whole/part relation, metonymy will include the figure of speech called "synechdoche": "hands" for workmen, "Britain" for the British government). These figures expose very vividly the working of proportional oppositions at the level of the word, before it enters into sentences. Jakobson was especially interested in the distinction as it appears in aphasia, between "similarity disorders," in which sentence structure is intact but words are selected wrongly on the paradigmatic plane, and "contiguity disorders," in which the right words are spoken in the wrong order. He remarked also how literary styles range between the poles of the metaphorical in some kinds of poetry (substituting the word with the richest similarities) and of the metonymic in realistic prose (picking the detail which carries the most context with it). One might notice also how returning from a holiday abroad one brings back as reminders of the country photographs (similar to the scene, therefore metaphoric), and perhaps a sari or a boomerang (attached to a context exclusive to India or to Australia, therefore metonymic). An example especially relevant to correlative thinking in cosmology, noticed by Jakobson, is the distinction between "imitative" and "contagious" magic. In order to destroy an enemy, one sticks pins in a wax image (which is similar to him) or steals hair or a glove to practise on (things contiguous to him); it is as though the magician were perfectly rational except in confusing the metaphoric and metonymic with the literal.

We may recognise the similar and the connected as having the same place in animal as in human intelligence. Pavlov's dog expects dinner as he hears the bell:

	A	Similarity	B
1.	Bells (before)		Bell (now)
2.	Food (before)		—

Connection

	A	Contrast	B
1.	Eating		Hunger
2.	Approach		Avoid

Connection

So the gap fills with the expectation of food, which in turn sets off the preparation to eat. There is no reason to suppose that humans in the same situation are reacting any differently even when they break out into speech, which will very probably consist of words not yet syntactically organised.

'The bell!'

'Ah, dinner, good.'

So far, the speakers accept uncritically the system of oppositions in which they respond with the unreflecting sureness of the animal. Having the capacity to form sentences, however, they are no longer restricted to expecting the connected when they hear the similar, they can shift attention to and test the similarity and the connection, ask whether it is the same bell or whether it is being rung for the usual reason.

It does not follow, however, that by manipulating sentences we can dissolve by a total analysis the proportional oppositions which distinguish the conceptual scheme of our own culture. We cannot without an infinite regress (analysing the similarities and connections assumed in analysis) get farther than the criticism and adjustment of relations which we find obscure or in conflict with logic or observation. The Chinese language is especially instructive here because of its proneness to expose chains of oppositions by laying them out and linking them in parallel clauses.

Huainanzi (ch. 16) Liu 16/2B

清之爲明，杯水見眸子。
濁之爲闇，河水不見太山。

'The clear being luminous, in a cup of water you see the pupil of the eye; the muddy being dark, in the water of the River you do not see Mount Tai.'

Here we have one chain in the preliminary and another in the main clause:

	A	B	A	B
1.	Clear	Muddy	Water in a cup	Water of the River
2.	Light	Dark	Pupil of eye	Mount Tai

The syntax is marked by word order and particles, but each main clause has an exposed element:

Exposed	*Verb*	*Object*
杯水	見	眸子
河水	不見	太山
Water in cup	see	pupil of eye
Water of River	not see	Mount Tai

The exposed element is related to verb and object solely by the proportional oppositions:

(1) *Paradigmatic* The water in a cup compares with the water of the River as the pupil with Mount Tai (as minute by contrast).

(2) *Syntagmatic* The water in a cup connects with seeing the pupil as the water of the River with seeing Mount Tai (as contiguous with the seen, what one sees it in).

In the second case the English translation makes the nature of the contiguity explicit by syntax. In the first, however, the English as much as the Chinese depends on the proportional oppositions; it would be pointless to expand the sentence to say explicitly "... you see even something as small as a pupil ... you do not see even something as big as Mount Tai." Any sentence, in Chinese or in English, is floated on a sea of unformulated similarities and contrasts.

Here we may pause to make clearer our divergence from the viewpoint of Granet.

Any serious inquirer into Chinese thought is on watch for differences between what we are accustomed to call the "conceptual schemes" of China and the West. To focus this search on contrasting chains of proportional oppositions helps to clarify what we mean by this vague term. But to treat Yin-Yang thinking as specifically *la pensée chinoise* is in effect to contrast the correlative stratum of thinking which is more fully exposed in China with the analytic upper layer which is thicker and denser in the West, confusing different levels. The Chinese chains of oppositions are indeed most visible in Yin-Yang cosmology; but for a view of our own conceptual scheme displayed with the same clarity, one must go not to Western logic and science but to the chain "God/Devil, Good/evil, Heaven/hell" of religion, or to those disreputable systems in the background of the rationalist tradition which come to look important only when the origins of modern science are discovered in Renaissance hermeticism and cabbalism, or of socialism in fantasts such as Fourier. In the philosophers on the other hand, whether

Chinese or Western, the correlative layer is submerged under the thinking which builds on it; if, for example, in struggling to understand Mencius, one seems to grasp a conceptual difference from Hobbes and Rousseau in an underlying assumption that "Man's nature : moral goodness :: the tendency of life : longevity,"[21] it is just as when Ryle perceives behind the Western mind/body dichotomy a mechanistic variation on "Mind : body :: ruler : subject."

3
PAIRS: THE YIN AND YANG

Classical Chinese is a language remarkable for the ease with which it moves between the rhythmically punctuated and parallelised clauses in which the thinker is grouping concepts in rows of pairs and the unequal and syntactically complex sentences in which he thinks with them. It shows up very clearly the difference between shaping a conceptual scheme and reasoning inside it. Granet already noticed the connection between the parallelistic style and Yin-Yang cosmology; writing at a time when little was known about Chinese grammar, he went so far as to assert that the Chinese language "has succeeded in reserving for rhythm alone the task of organising the expression of thought."[22]

Nowadays, after some 50 years of rather modest progress in analysing the syntax which was almost invisible to Granet ("Some particles, which in any case each serve more than one purpose, and function primarily for oral punctuation, help to make the meaning of the phrase comprehensible"),[23] we would see the connection a little differently. The parallelistic style flourishes with the thriving of Yin-Yang cosmology during the Han; but throughout the literature of the classical period, before philosophers paid attention to cosmology, parallelism is subordinate to syntax. Even *Laozi*, in the manuscripts of the 2nd century BCE discovered at Mawangdui, is as rich in particles as any other pre-Han text.

The tendency to parallelism is characteristic not only of correlative thinking but of philosophical criticism of correlations, as in the *Xiaoqu* 小取 chapter of *Mozi* and, within the limits imposed by English syntax, in Gilbert Ryle's *Concept of mind*. The *Xiaoqu* criticises the claim "Robbers are people, killing robbers is killing people" (*sha ren* 殺人,

which has the pejorative meaning of "murder, massacre"). It recognises behind the claim a mistaken assumption that "killing people" is parallel to such a phrase as "riding horses" in which the meanings of words remain unaltered in combination – that is, it rejects the correlation "kill : people :: ride : horses." Its procedure is to run a series of sentences parallel.

獲之親人也,獲事其親非事人也。其弟美人也,愛弟非愛美人也……世相與共是之。若若是,則雖盜人人也,愛盜非愛人也,不愛盜非不愛人也,殺盜人非殺人也,無難矣。

'Huo's parent is someone, but Huo's serving her parent is not serving someone (*shi ren* "serving a husband"). Her younger brother is a handsome man, but loving her younger brother is not loving a handsome man (loving him for his looks) … The whole world agrees that these are right; but if such is the case, there is no difficulty in allowing that, although robbers are people, loving robbers is not loving people (*ai ren* "loving mankind"), not loving robbers is not not loving people, killing robbers is not killing people (*sha ren* "murder").'

When Ryle points out differences between tasks (aiming, treating, scanning) and achievements (hitting, curing, seeing), overlooked when we assume them to be "co-ordinate species of activity or process," his style falls into the same kind of parallelism.

"This is why we can significantly say that someone has aimed in vain or successfully, but not that he has hit the target in vain or successfully; that he has treated his patient assiduously or unassiduously, but not that he has cured him assiduously or unassiduously; that he scanned the hedgerow slowly or rapidly, systematically or haphazardly, but not that he saw the nest slowly or rapidly, systematically or haphazardly."[24]

Whichever position we take on the disputed issue of whether all thinking is ultimately binary, there can be no doubt of the centrality of binary oppositions in Chinese culture. Everywhere from the pairs and sets of four, five or more in cosmology to the parallelism of prose and the tone patterns of regulated verse, we find groups which, even when the number is odd, divide neatly into pairs with one left over. The traditional cosmology as it settles into its lasting shape in the 3rd century BCE is ordered by lining up all binary oppositions along a single chain, with one member Yin and the other Yang. The *Cheng* 稱, one of the additional documents on Mawangdui manuscript B of *Laozi* provides the earliest comprehensive list of which we know.

凡論必以陰陽明大義。天陽地陰……

'Whenever sorting, be sure to use the Yin and Yang to make plain the grand scheme. Heaven is Yang, Earth is Yin ....'[25]

The list continues in parallel phrases on the same model ("X is Yang, Y is Yin").

	A *Yang*	B *Yin*	Paradigm
1.	Heaven	Earth	
2.	Spring	Autumn	
3.	Summer	Winter	
4.	Day	Night	
5.	Big states	Small states	
6.	Important states	Insignificant states	
7.	Action	Inaction	
8.	Stretching	Contracting	
9.	Ruler	Minister	
10.	Above	Below	
11.	Man	Woman	
12.	Father	Child	
13.	Elder brother	Younger brother	
14.	Older	Younger	
15.	Noble	Base	
16.	Getting on in the world	Being stuck where one is	
17.	Taking a wife, begetting a child	Having a funeral	
18.	Controlling others	Being controlled by others	
19.	Guest	Host	
20.	Soldiers	Labourers	
21.	Speech	Silence	
22.	Giving	Receiving	

Syntagm

Throughout the chain, A is superior to B but the two are mutually dependent; it does not, like the illustrative series with which our argument started, lead to "Good/evil." As has long been recognised, China tends to treat opposites as complementary, the West as conflicting. It is the explicitness of the Yin-Yang system which shows up this difference, the first between the conceptual schemes of the two traditions to attract attention. That his own oppositions tend likewise to run in a chain is less obvious to a Westerner. But, since the post-structuralist Derrida pointed out the links, one begins to see an affinity, for example, between the Christian faith in the immortality of the soul and the scientist's (before quantum mechanics) in universal causation; given the pairs "Life/death" and "Necessity/chance," the West strives to abolish B and preserve only A.

In both China and the West one finds correlation between the universe as macrocosm and man as microcosm. We shall take examples from Kepler's *Epitome of Copernican Astronomy* (which, in spite of his three planetary laws, belongs not to modern but to mediaeval cosmology) and from ch. 3 and 7 of *Huainanzi*. For the ancient Chinese, Heaven with its revolving luminaries is round like the head, Earth spreading in the Four Directions is rectangular like the feet;

similarly for Kepler the curved represents God and the rectilinear His creatures, and since the most perfect rectilinear figures are the five regular solids, the distances between the planets correspond to their proportions, starting with the cube, tetrahedron and dodecahedron, since (it is as though Kepler was waiting to be analysed by a structuralist), "in these figures there appears the first of the metaphysical oppositions, that between the same and the other, or the different."[26]

Kepler	*Huainanzi* (ch. 3, 7)	Liu 3/30A	7/2A, 3A
A	B	A	B
Faculties of soul	Perfections of world	1. Heaven 2. Earth	Head Feet
Sensitive	Light	3. Four seasons	Four limbs
Vital	Heat	4. 12 months	12 joints
Animal	Movement	5. Sun and moon	Ears and eyes
Rational	Harmony	6. Wind and rain	Blood and *qi*

In the proportional oppositions of *Huainanzi*, Heaven connects with Earth as head with feet (the former above the latter), the Four Seasons connect with the 12 months as the four limbs with their 12 joints (the former containing the latter). On the paradigmatic plane, Heaven compares with head as Earth with feet, as similar in being above, allowing the possibility of using one as metaphor for the other. Kepler in fact writes: "The adornment of the world consists in light; its life and growth in heat; and, so to speak, its action in movement; and its contemplation – wherein Aristotle places blessedness – in harmonies."[27] He also, at a point where his correlations approach *Huainanzi*'s Position 5, says the sun "is as if the eye of the world."[28]

Let us now take the plunge into the most developed cosmogony in early Chinese literature, at the beginning of the astronomical chapter of *Huainanzi* (ch. 3). In translating, we italicise all sentences beginning with "Therefore."

Huainanzi (Ch. 3) Liu 3/1A–2B (Emendations follow Liu's notes)

天墜未形,馮馮翼翼,洞洞灟灟,故曰太(昭)＊始。道始于虛霩,虛霩生宇宙,宇宙生氣。氣有涯垠,清陽(＝揚)者薄靡而爲天,重濁者凝滯而爲地。清妙之合專易,重濁之凝竭難,故天先成而地後定。天地之襲精爲陰陽,陰陽之專精爲四時,四時之散精爲萬物。積陽之熱氣生火,火氣之精者爲日;積陰之寒氣爲水,水氣之精者爲月。日月之淫爲精者爲星辰,天受日月星辰,地受水潦塵埃。……

天道曰圓,地道曰方,方者主幽,圓者主明。明者吐氣者也,是故火(日)＊日外景。幽者含氣者也,是故水(日)＊月內景。吐氣者施,含氣者化,是故陽施陰化。天〈地〉之偏氣怒者爲風,〈天〉地之(含)＊合氣和者爲雨。陰陽相薄感而爲雷,激而爲霆,亂而爲霧。陽氣勝則散而爲雨露,陰氣勝則凝而爲霜雪。毛羽者飛行之類也,故屬於陽,介鱗者蟄伏之類也,故屬於陰。日者陽之主也,是故春夏則羣獸除,日至而麋鹿解。月者陰之宗也,是以月虛而魚腦減,月死而蠃蚌膲。火上蕁,水下流,故鳥飛而高,魚動而下。物類相動，本標相應，故陽燧見日則燃而爲火，方諸見月則津而爲水。

'When Heaven and Earth were not yet shaped, it was amorphous, vague, a blank, a blur; *call it, therefore, "The Primal Beginning."* The Way began in the tenuous and transparent, the tenuous and transparent generated Space and Time, Space and Time generated the *qi*. There was a shoreline in the *qi*; the clear and soaring dissipated to become Heaven, the heavy and muddy congealed to become Earth. The concentration of the clear and subtle is easy, the concretion of the heavy and muddy is difficult; *therefore, Heaven was completed first and Earth afterwards.*

'The superimposed quintessences of Heaven and Earth became the Yang and Yin, the concentrating quintessences of Yin and Yang became the Four Seasons, the scattering quintessences of the Four Seasons became the myriad creatures. The hot *qi* of the accumulating Yang generated fire, the quintessence of the *qi* of fire became the sun; the cold *qi* of the accumulating Yin became water, the quintessence of the *qi* of water became the moon; the overflow of the quintessences of sun and moon became the stars. Heaven received the sun, moon and stars, Earth received the showers of water and the dust and dirt.'

After a mythological interlude to explain corresponding asymmetries of Heaven and Earth, the account continues with an elliptical reference to the unimpeded motion of the circular Heaven and the immobility of the square Earth.

'The Way of Heaven one calls "round," the Way of Earth one calls "square." It is primary to the square to retreat to the dark, primary to the round to illuminate. To illuminate is to expel *qi*, *for which reason fire and sun cast the image outside*. To retreat to the dark is to hold *qi* in, *for which reason water and moon draw the image inside*. What expels *qi* does *to*, what holds *qi* in is transformed *by*. Therefore, *the Yang does to, the Yin is transformed by*.

'Of the *qi* inclining to Heaven, the raging

became wind; of the combining *qi* of Heaven and Earth, the harmonious became rain. When Yin and Yang clashed, being roused they became thunder, crossing paths they became lightning, confusing they became mist. When the Yang *qi* prevailed, it scattered to become rain and dew; when the Yin *qi* prevailed, it congealed to become frost and snow.

'The furred and feathered are the kinds which fly and run, *and therefore belong to the Yang*; the shelled and the scaly are the kinds which hibernate and hide, *and therefore belong to the Yin*. The sun is ruler of the Yang, and *for this reason in spring and summer the herd animals shed hair, and at the solstice the deer throw off their horns*; the moon is forebear of the Yin, *which is why when the moon wanes the brains of fishes diminish, and when the moon dies the swollen oyster shrinks.*

'Fire goes up and trails, water goes down and flows, *therefore the birds flying up go high, the fish when stirred go down*. Things which are of a kind stir each other, what is at the root and what are at the tips respond to each other. *Therefore, when the Yang burner* [concave mirror] *sees the sun, it ignites and makes fire; when the square "zhu"* [an object laid out at night to catch the dew] *sees the moon, it moistens and makes water.*'

Further examples follow, but these will be enough. The cosmos is seen as evolving by division along a chain of binary oppositions. The Tao as "Way," course, path, introduces the first opposition between the amorphous as spatially extended and as temporally enduring, so that it becomes the mobile *qi* "air, breath," the *qi*, which we experience as the influences from the atmosphere and in the body which brighten or darken, activate or clog, divides into "clear/muddy" (*qing* 清/*zhuo* 濁, used primarily of water), and with the rising of the clear and sinking of the muddy becomes Heaven and Earth. From this point onwards we notice the clauses falling into parallel pairs. *Huainanzi* orders the similarities and differences of its cosmos by taking crucial binary oppositions, as they are drawn in Chinese culture, and identifying the sequence which shapes the simplest and yet most comprehensive pattern. In tabulating the oppositions our numbering will for the first time be marking a fixed succession. The table will also be the first to differentiate nominal and verbal concepts; we shall distinguish the former by capitals.

QI

	A	B	Paradigm
1.	Clear and subtle	Heavy and muddy	
2.	HEAVEN	EARTH	
3.	YANG	YIN	
4.	Hot	Cold	
5.	FIRE	WATER	
6.	SUN	MOON	
7.	Round	Square	
8.	Illuminates	Retreats to dark	
9.	Expels	Holds in	
10.	Does to	Is transformed by	
11.	Scatters	Congeals	
12.	RAIN and DEW	FROST and SNOW	
13.	FURRED and FEATHERED	SHELLED and SCALY	
14.	Flies or runs	Hibernates or hides	
15.	Goes up	Goes down	

Syntagm

Throughout the table, A and B contrast as parallel structures, with the same connections at every joint.

Positions 1, 2 The clear becomes Heaven, the muddy becomes Earth.

Positions 3, 5 Yang *generates* fire, Yin generates water.

Positions 5, 6 Sun *is quintessence of* fire, moon is quintessence of water.

Positions 5, 15 Fire rises, water sinks; "fire/water" and "rise/sink" share the connection of agent and action.

Positions 1, 11, 15 The causal connections between being clear, rising and scattering are unspecified, but the same as those between being muddy, sinking and congealing.

Within the parallel structures, verbal concepts specify respects in which on the one hand nominal A and B contrast and on the other nominal 1, 2 ... are similar.

Positions 4–6 Fire in being hot is unlike water but like sun, water in being cold is unlike fire but like moon.

With the specifying of the respects, correlative thinking becomes explicit; it is no longer just the spontaneous formation of a *Gestalt*. The cosmologist is in effect trying to lay out before us the whole system of paradigmatic and syntagmatic relations which *Gestalt* insight and analogical and analytic thinking assume but leave implicit. The great interest of such system-building, we suggested in the *Introduction*, is that it is the only kind of thinking which makes this try at bringing everything submerged to the surface. The result is a coherent but of course very simplified scheme. He is now equipped to explain why startled birds fly up and fish dive down, not by isolated analogies, but by similarities and contrasts throughout the total scheme; if fire contrasts with water in that one goes up and the other down, and birds contrast with fish as fire with water, then birds like fire will go up and fish like water will go down. It is not that the cosmologist is applying a *theory* about Yin and Yang; for purposes of explanation and inference, "Yang" and "Yin" function like our "A" and "B," they mark the series with which something connects and the opposite series with a member of which it contrasts.

But once imprisoned in formulae, correlative thinking loses its capacity for fine discriminations and assimilations. There is indeed a rough similarity running down each column of the table, enough to give a meaning to "Yin" and "Yang," commonly described in English as the active and passive or positive and negative principles; but all in all the similarity is a Wittgensteinian "family resemblance," by which 1 can be like 2, and 2 like 3, without 1 being like 3. What the system of correspondences does retain of the correlative thinking of practical life is precisely what post-Galilean science strives to escape, the incompleteness of explanations which assume interrelations with all parts of an indefinitely limited structure. Should one ask why, if square connects with moon as round with sun, the moon is not square, one would be expected to look higher up the chain and take into account that moon like sun connects with Heaven (round) as water and soil with Earth (square). Every explanation, therefore, is modifiable from elsewhere in an indefinitely extendable pattern, permitting a licence which the cosmologist tries to restrict by the principle that the higher in the chain is "ruler" (*zhu* 主) or "ancestor" (*zong* 宗) of the lower.

Among the sentences introduced by a "Therefore" (*gu* 故, *shi gu* 是故, *shi yi* 是以), we shall ignore the cosmologist's reason at the start for speaking of the "Primal Beginning," as well as a genuine causal explanation (Heaven took shape before Earth because the heavy takes longer to come together than the rarefied) and an unimpeachable deduction (the Yang illuminates, "to illuminate is to expel *qi*," "what expels does *to*," and "therefore the Yang does *to*"). Each correlative explanation presents what is seen as the crucial among the indefinite number of factors bearing on the case, very much as we pick out the crucial factor in offering a causal explanation. We shall supply from the total scheme what we take to be the other most relevant factors. It may be noticed that the conclusion is always a contrastive pair which could be added to the chain of oppositions. The scheme explains connections (becoming, generating, concave mirror interacting with sun and fire) only by similarity to or contrast with other connections.

Question 1. Why do fire and sun radiate their glow and cast shadows outside, moon and water contain their glow and draw shadows within?

(*Ying* 景＝影 "glow, shadow," here translated "image," is what shows up as light against dark or dark against light. *Yue* 月 "moon" is here a conjectural emendation; the *jin* 金 "metal" of the parallel (故火日外景而金水內景) in *Da Daili* 大戴禮 ch. 58 perhaps suits the argument better, since metal not only glows but reflects.)

Answer Because to illuminate is to expel *qi*, to retreat to the dark is to hold *qi* in.

Assumed factors Water retreats to the dark as fire illuminates (Positions 5, 8). It tends in the opposite direction to fire, sinks as fire rises, hides in Earth as fire flies towards Heaven (Positions 2, 14, 15). Unless changed by the action of fire, it is cold not hot, congeals rather than scatters, becomes frost and snow not rain and dew (Positions 4, 11, 12, cf. 10), so holds *qi* in as fire shoots it out. As for sun and moon, they have been pronounced the quintessences of fire and water.

Question 2. Why are animals and birds Yang, invertebrates and fish Yin?

Answer Because the former run and fly, the latter hibernate and hide.

Assumed factors Running and flying compare with hibernating and hiding as shining with retreating from light, expelling with retaining, going up with sinking down (A8, 9, 15 Yang with B8, 9, 15, Yin). The furred and feathered would also compare with the shelled and scaly as scattering with congealing, hot with cold (A4, 11 Yang, B4, 11 Yin).

Question 3. Why do animals throw off hair and horns as the sun advances in the early year and the fish and oyster shrink as the moon wanes in the late month?

Answer Because the sun is ruler of Yang things and the moon ancestor of Yin things.

Assumed factors Animals (Yang) differ from fish (Yin) as sun from moon, animals resemble sun as fish moon (Positions 6, 13). Since the sun and moon are the dominant pair, in the seasons of advancing sun animals get hotter, expel and scatter (Positions 4, 9, 11) like the sun, but the sun does not fly up like a bird (Position 14); and in the last half of the month fish and oysters shrink like the moon but the moon does not dive down like a fish. This is the only one of the arguments which shifts one side (B) a little off the explicit chain of oppositions.

Question 4. Why when disturbed do birds fly up but fish dive down?

Answer Because fire goes up and water goes down.

Assumed factors Birds differ from fish as fire from water, birds resemble fire as fish water (Positions 5, 13). In what respects? Birds like fire connect with light and with the thinner *qi* which rises to become Heaven, fish like water with darkness and the thicker *qi* which sinks to become Earth (Positions 1, 2, 8). This argument follows directly on to the last and again assumes the dominance of fire and water or their quintessences the sun and moon.

Question 5. Why does the Yang mirror draw fire from the sun and the square *zhu* draw dew from the moon?

Answer Because "things of a kind (in being Yin or being Yang) stir each other, the root and the tip respond to each other."

Assumed factors In the interaction of the

three, the Yang or concave mirror (being Yang not only in name but by being round, Position 7) connects with the sun which is quintessence of fire as the *zhu* (square, therefore Yin, Position 7) connects with the moon which is quintessence of water (Positions 5, 6). That the interacting things are opposites explains why they interact in opposite ways (*how* they interact is seen as irrelevant). This is the only argument which connects nominal concepts with each other, not with verbal concepts which relate them as similar or different. Concave mirror, sun and fire are "of a kind" in belonging to the A column, are "root" or "tip" according to their higher or lower position in the chain.

Throughout these arguments it is never *said* that anything is similar to or different from anything else (although the cosmologist does refer to *lei* 類 "kinds"). To shift similarity/difference from the paradigmatic to the syntagmatic plane and say "X is like/unlike Y," as Chinese thinkers do often enough outside cosmology, is to move away from correlative towards analytic thinking.

The enterprise of unifying phenomena by stringing all binary oppositions on a single chain as Yin and Yang implies treating the differences between A and B and similarities between 1, 2, 3 … as in the same respects throughout. The effect is to sharpen contrasts but blur connections. Contrast pushes towards describing by the more similar of polar opposites, a metaphoric shift (fire illuminates, water *retreats to the dark*); connections blend in the direction of identity as in metonymy (fire rises, by metonymy birds are fire, therefore birds rise). But this forcing of phenomena into too simple a frame does not imply that the thinking is illogical or "pre-logical." Correlative thinking assumes a principle which we might formulate as follows:

'The more the similarities within and differences between parallel structures, the more there are likely to be.'

If this raises a logical difficulty, it is the same as the one which worries logicians in the principle of induction:

'The more instances for which a generalisation holds, the more likely that it holds for all.'

Thus in noting the many structurally related respects in which two or more lobsters outwardly resemble each other and differ from two or more frogs, one could infer from the opened ones what the unopened are like inside, with as good reason as in deducing from generalisations about the species based on the same number of specimens. The *Huainanzi* cosmologist thinks that he discerns parallel structures with indefinite limits in which the salient connections might be clarified as follows:

Birds live in	Fish live in
the thinner *qi*	the thicker *qi*
which rises	which sinks
as Heaven,	as Earth,
of which the hot *qi*	of which the cold *qi*
generates fire.	generates water.
Fire illuminates.	Water retreats to dark.
Birds approach the light,	Fish approach the dark,
Fire rises.	Water sinks.
Birds fly up.	Fish dive down.

The cosmologist thinks that the last of the phenomena is explained by its relation to the rest (as the frog having bones in its leg and the lobster not is explained by the relation to the rest of the body). The objection would be, not that one cannot use structural parallelism for explanation, but that as soon as one learns to discount connections which are not causal the impression of structural parallelism turns out to be illusory.

In exploring proto-scientific thinking it has been usual to start from what we find peculiar in pre-modern views of nature; here we have followed the example of Lévi-Strauss (although not the detail of his methods) in starting from the opposite direction, from structures common to pre-modern and modern thinking. To infer correlatively how nominal concepts inter-connect is (except when equating them by such a word as *wei* 爲 "be, become") to think of the things as interacting; there is no need to assume that the Chinese cosmologists thought correlatively *because* they conceived the cosmos as an organism. In the large area of ordinary life which is too complex and transient to be unravelled by analysis, so that we have to trust to spontaneous expectations springing from the immediate perception of pattern, we likewise see ourselves as involved in a multiplicity of interacting factors. In the fluid patterning of shifting experience the thinker is on the near side of his analytically ordered information; on the far side is the immense realm which, before the time of Galileo, could be reduced to order only by the same kind of patterning. Out there, however, correlative thinking loses the assurance and suppleness with which we exercise it in practical life. On the near side, it is disciplined to an art by the recurrent defeat of expectation in urgent situations; on the far side, obstacles to the flight of fancy are weaker and fewer. On the near side, subtle discriminations and assimilations can draw a constantly veering line between the similar and the different, unhampered by verbal formulation; on the far side, the rigidity of schemes is equalled by the licence in applying them. On the near, there is too much information to be confined by any system, on the far too little to correct any system.

Putting aside the disputed issue of whether all thinking is at bottom binary, one may notice that the binary tends to leave out the maker of the opposition. "Left/right," "above/below," "before/after" (not however "I/you," "here/there," "now/then") imply a spatial or temporal centre from which the opposition is drawn, inviting the expansion of the pair to a triad. Thus in China the pair Heaven above and Earth below grows towards the end of the classical period to Heaven, Earth and Man. Kepler too has a taste for triads, with ourselves living on the third member (the planets, among which Earth is itself a third, being located between the correlatives of the primary and secondary regular solids). The symmetry of the following table provides one of the proofs by which the heliocentric theory came to be established at the beginning of modern science.[29]

	A	B	*Between/within*
(God)	Father	Son	Holy Spirit
(Sphere)	Centre	Surface	Intermediate space
(Universe)	Sun	Stars	Planets

Such a correlation is convincing to Kepler because it applies oppositions commonly accepted within the Christian tradition. Within the Trinity, Father and Son are the pair, outside the believer and visualisable by him; the Holy Spirit, who in the words of the Creed "proceeds from the Father and the Son," is experienced as infusing divine grace from within. The earth stands between Heaven and Hell, which for Aquinas and other Mediaeval theologians had been geographically as well as spiritually above and below. The latter triad relates to a chain without a third place which in both China and the West is more deeply rooted than either Christianity or Yin-Yang cosmology:

	A	B
1.	Heaven	Earth
2.	Above	Below
3.	Ruler	Subject
4.	Better	Worse

In West and East alike, the opposition "superior/inferior," *shang* 上 *xia* 下, metonymically fuses spatial and moral elevation. The relation is not of similarity (in which case it would be not metonymic but metaphorical) but of connection; the physical act of looking upward at the king on his throne or dictator on his podium disposes one to respond as his inferior.

Here we have another difference from post-Galilean science. That [which]* has no "Between/within" can take account of the subjective only by objectivising it. The computer continues untroubled through its binary operations without noticing itself.

---

*Publisher's note: this corrects a lacuna in the original text.

4
FOURS AND FIVES:
THE FIVE PHASES

Turning now to larger sets, they tend to lack the apparent inevitability of binary oppositions. This inevitability is of course culture-bound, but even a Westerner with some experience of Chinese thought can generally guess which of a pair is Yin and which Yang; he is seldom so lucky in correlating the Five Phases with the Five Notes or the Five Tastes. In China too the Five Phases were never as deeply rooted in the philosophical tradition as the Yin and Yang. Larger sets are also harder to fit to the facts and to develop consistently. We may illustrate the point from two conflicting sets in the European symbolism of colours.

(A) Colours of races, deriving from the binary "white : black :: good : evil."

	A	B	C	D	E
1.	White	Yellow	Red	Brown	Black
2.	Lightest	Less light	?	Less dark	Darkest
3.	Good	Less good	?	Less evil	Evil

(B) The colourful as the vivid, the vital, deriving from the binary "colourful : pale :: life : death."

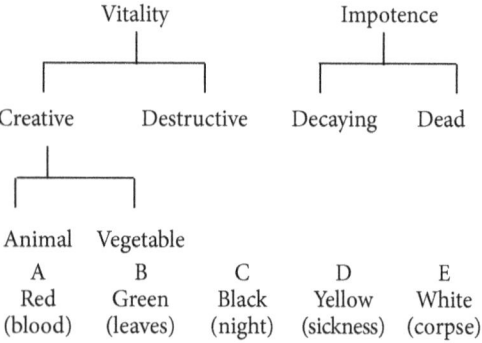

We might derive both structures from a common "light/darkness," but in developing they contradict each other, the contradiction centring on the colour white. The white man is predisposed by them to think of other races as inferior to the degree that they recede from his own norm of colour, but also as more intensely alive. To some extent the contradiction fits in rather well with the conflict between the spontaneous and the good in the Christian doctrine of Original Sin, for which the vitality of nature is temptation. It is then reconcilable to see the black man as both the most savage and the most seductively potent. The red man, historically the latest to be discovered, has been assigned a colour which does not fit neatly into the first series. Consequently, although undoubtedly dark enough to be identified as inferior, he can draw from the second series the creative vitality of red blood to turn him into a superior kind of savage; in the Western imagination the Red Indian is indeed the main candidate for the role of the Noble Savage, with the Polynesian as his only rival among the brown races. Similarly, when classifying women by the colour of their hair, the fiery redhead stands outside the scale from virginally innocent blonde to sultry and dangerous brunette. The albino of course presents no difficulty. He belongs to the second series, because it is logically impossible for the whiter than the best to be better, and because his complexion is in any case against nature.

We may notice how loosely the colour classifications fit, compared with the binary oppositions we have listed. Naming is by contrast within the scheme rather than by adequacy to the object. The Mongol is to the eye often whiter than the Caucasian, American Indians are red because the brown people live in Asia and Polynesia. The ease with which one classifies peoples, indeed *sees* them as they are conventionally supposed to be coloured, helps one to understand why schemes in other cultures, which to ourselves seem obviously artificial, are so resistant to conflicting observation. We may add that our more complex second structure lacks the firm lines of the first, leaving scope to expand it and make it looser still. The single association we have bracketed after each colour does not of course exhaust its significance, which is multiple, indefinite and variable between individuals even in Western culture; thus red (bloodshed, fire) threatens to burst out of its allotted place to join black in the compartment for destructive vitality. Both series stand out from our other illustrations by their pre-conscious, glaringly irrational character. From Kepler we have travelled to a level of the mind halfway back to Pavlov's dog, tracing a structural affinity between all three. "Black" becomes a pure metonym for "Evil," reducing to identity a connection which even those most under its influence seldom consciously maintain to be causal.

An activity in which correlative thinking breaks away from such systems is creation and appreciation in the arts. Even those who identify the correlative with pre-scientific thinking still acknowledge its relevance to Beauty if not to Truth. Indeed, as science progresses, artists seem to become more rather than less inclined to the primitivism for which they are excused. Baudelaire's *Les correspondances* is a sonnet about correlative thinking itself, Rimbaud's on the colours of the vowels is explicitly an exercise in it; and both verses were founding documents of the Symbolist movement from which modernism in poetry began. Yeats' prolonged maturation as a poet is a demonstration that a fine mind can, not deteriorate, but flourish on the degenerate systems of occultism. The function of correlative thinking in the arts is not, however, a mere matter of weaving beautiful patterns disconnected from truth. Remote as it is from scientific thinking, it may be seen as itself a criticism of correlative system-building, a revision of fossilised chains of oppositions in the light of closer scrutiny of the object. It takes another course than the scientific by retaining that "Between" where the observer interacts with the rest, not excluding the subjective response, not abjuring metaphor and metonym, but far from reverting to primitivism it re-patterns experience by a style of thinking more fluid, intricate and finely discriminating than any other. It tells its own kind of truth by revealing how one does spontaneously, therefore genuinely, react in the fullest awareness of a concrete situation.

However, its structure does not cease to be that which we have been analysing, a point we may illustrate from Conrad's story *Heart of darkness*. We pick out from its texture a minor strand which relates aptly to previous illustrations leading back to "Yang/Yin," "Light/darkness."

Conrad's story dissolves conceptual schemes by starting from an opposition between concrete scenes, "River Thames/River Congo," and letting the chain take its own course whether in accord with or against the conflicting oppositions "white : black :: good : evil," "colourful : pale :: life : death," integrating with both in an intricate new pattern.

A	B
Thames	Congo
Gloom	Glaring sun
City	Dark forest
Civilised	Savage
Artificial	True
Progress	The primaeval
Clarity	Mystery
White	Black

The "light/darkness" opposition introduced in the title of the story settles into place only when A and B intermingle.

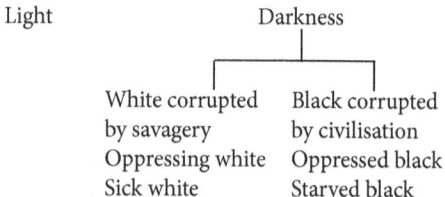

Light	Darkness	
	White corrupted by savagery	Black corrupted by civilisation
	Oppressing white	Oppressed black
	Sick white	Starved black

The simple "black/white" of the races adjusts in the course of the story to the complex "bronze/ivory," the bronze skins of the tribe at the end of the journey allying them with both sun and night (with the foremost tribesmen painted red), and the hairless head of the sick Kurtz become ivory, the dead matter from a living animal in pursuit of which he has lost his soul. As for the "Between," it is the narrator beginning his story in the calm evening light in a boat between river and sea, from a viewpoint which embraces a further opposition detaching moral from physical complexion ("African : European :: ancient Briton : Roman").

A	B	*Between*
Audience	Kurtz	Narrator
England	Unnamed destination	Mouth of Thames
Dazzle	Darkness	Calm light
Day	Night	Evening

(The unnamed destination is the zero of linguistics, meaningful by contrast).

We may see thinking in the arts as intermediate between the pre-consciousness of "white : black :: good : evil" and the full consciousness of explicit schemes of correspondences, Kepler's or Zou Yan's. Artists of course vary greatly in the extent to which they analyse their own effects, which like the extent to which scientists' creative thinking is correlative belongs to biography and not to the appreciation of their work. One does not, in analysing *Heart of darkness*, care whether Conrad himself would have agreed that he was contrasting bronze bodies with the ivory head of Kurtz.

Lévi-Strauss has remarked on the resemblance of correlative schemes of preliterate cultures to those of 'the naturalists and hermetics of antiquity and of the Middle Ages, Galen, Pliny, Hermes Trismegistus, Albertus Magnus.'[30] As a sample from outside China, we take this one from the Hopis.[31]

	A	B	C
(Directions)	NW	SW	SE
(Colours)	Yellow	Blue/green	Red
(Animals)	Puma	Bear	Wild Cat
(Birds)	Oriole	Bluebird	Parakeet
	D	E	F
(Directions)	NE	Zenith	Nadir
(Colours)	White	Black	Multicoloured
(Animals)	Wolf	Vulture	Snake
(Birds)	Magpie	Swallow	Warbler

The earliest schemes documented in China are in the various calendars regulating the ruler's conduct throughout the year. The standard one is in the *Lüshi chunqiu* (c. 240 BCE) from which it passed into the Confucian tradition as the *Monthly Orders* (*Yueling* 月令) in the *Book of Rites*. While pairs are correlated with Yin and Yang, sets of four or five are correlated with what this text calls "Powers" (*de* 德), those of wood, fire, soil, metal and water. Zou Yan also called them the "Five Powers." For reasons explained in the Appendix, I shall avoid the term *Wu xing* 五行, out of currency during this crucial period; it is current and interpretable as the "Five Phases" from the Han onwards, but in earlier usage seems to refer to the "Five Processes" specific to the materials, fire flaming and rising, water wetting and sinking, and so forth. Zou Yan about 250 BCE had explained the rises and falls of dynasties by the sequence in which the Five Powers conquer each other:

> Water (which extinguishes fire),
> Fire (which melts metal),
> Metal (which cuts wood),
> Wood (which digs earth),
> Soil (which dams water).

Their full co-ordination with the other fours and fives is not attested before the *Lüshi chunqiu*; the *Guanzi* miscellany has probably older calendrical schemes in which they are missing, or attached in a subsidiary position, or fitted to five divisions of the year without correlations.[32] Their co-ordination with times of year required the sequence in which the Five Powers generate each other:

> Wood (which catches fire),
> Fire (which reduces to ash),
> Soil (in which metals form),
> Metal (which liquefies when melted),
> Water (which nourishes wood).

We first consider the structural relations of the more easily analysable of the *Lüshi chunqiu* series (tastes and smells, for example, are too indefinite and affected by subjective influences for the Five Tastes and Five Smells to be usable for our purposes).

	A	B	Between	C	D
Five Powers	Wood	Fire	Soil	Metal	Water
Their numbers	8	7	5	9	6
Four Seasons	Spring	Summer	—	Autumn	Winter
Four Directions	East	South	(Centre)	West	North
Five Colours	Green	Red	Yellow	White	Black
Five Creatures	Scaly	Feathered	Naked	Furred	Shelled
Five Notes	Jue	Zhi	Gong	Shang	Yu

The numbers follow the enumeration (differently ordered) in the *Hongfan* 洪範 of the *Book of Documents*, continued into a second cycle to place 5 between 1 to 4 and 6 to 9.[33]

Water	Fire	Wood	Metal	Soil
1	2	3	4	5
6	7	8	9	

The reason for the choice of higher numbers was no doubt practical. Thus in the Mohist military chapters the divination of auspices when defending a city requires colours and numbers corresponding to the direction of the attack; in the case of attack from the North, it is plain that the number 1 would not do for 6.

Mozi HY 68/5–7
敵以北方來，迎之北壇。壇高六尺，堂密六。年六十者六人主祭。黑旗黑神，長六尺者六，弩六，六發而止。將服必黑，其牲以彘。

'When the enemy comes from the North, prepare to meet him with an altar on the North, the altar six feet high, the *mi* (?) of the hall six, with six men aged 60 in charge of the sacrifice, black flags and black gods, six of each six-feet high, six crossbows and a fusillade of six shots. The general's dress must be black, the victim a pig.'

The central column of the five represents the one left over from binary division, and in most cases is recognisable as the position from which the oppositions are perceived: the soil in which the other materials are grounded, the number five midway between one and nine, the centre from which one sees in the Four Directions (itself in later terminology included in the *Wu fang* 五方 "Five Directions"), the creature without scales, feathers, fur or shell which is man, and the Gong note fundamental to the pentatonic scale. There is none for the Four Seasons because the only temporal centre corresponding to "we" and "here" is "now." The *Lüshi chunqiu* shirks this difficulty by simply appending the correlations for the non-existent season at the end of the sixth month, the last of summer. The calendar in *Huainanzi* ch. 5 takes the desperate step of detaching the sixth month from summer as a separate season.

In inferring from sets of fives, it is not that one is applying a theory about the Five Powers, any more than one applies a theory about Yin and Yang to binary oppositions. Inferences are from similarity to others in a series, which the name of a Power identifies like the letters at the top of our columns. The basic correlation is of the Four Seasons with the Four Directions. Within both there is a proportional opposition:

	A	C	Paradigm	A	C
1.	Spring	Autumn		East	West
	B	D		B	D
2.	Summer	Winter		South	North

Syntagm

(Spring compares with autumn as summer with winter, spring connects with summer as autumn with winter).

The two sets correlate because in both of them A/C and B/D are the opposite positions of the sun in its recurring cycles, its temporal positions through the year and its spatial through the day. Following Chinese practice we put North at the bottom:

		B		
		South Summer		
A	East Spring	Centre	West Autumn	C
		North Winter		
		D		

Thinking which starts from this correlation will already be predisposed to conceive Heaven as round and Earth as square, following a chain which we might simplify as follows:

	A	B
1.	Heaven	Earth
2.	Motion round cardinal points	Rest at cardinal points
3.	Round	Square

The fitting of the Five Powers to the scheme seems at first sight quite arbitrary, but once it is recognised that they have to fall into two pairs and a remainder can be seen to be bound by the structural relations. The numbers ascribed to them since the *Hongfan* firmly identify the pairs:

1/2	3/4	5
6/7	8/9	
Water/fire	Wood/metal	Soil

Even without the numbers, "water/fire" is a solidly established pair throughout the early literature; we have already noticed it in the *Huainanzi* cosmogony (which ignored the other three), and it is the only one shared by the Five Powers and the symbols of the Eight Trigrams in the *Changes*. Soil is plainly destined for the isolated central position: wood grows in it, fire rises from it, metal is buried in it, water sinks into it. The other pair would therefore have to be "wood/metal." We saw in discussing the *Huainanzi* cosmogony that as the opposite of fire it is in the virtue of water to withdraw into the dark and the cold, so that the fitting of "fire/water" to "summer/winter" would seem inevitable. One can imagine that at this point the further observation that "wood/metal" contrast as "spring/autumn" (branches and leaves grow in spring and turn rigid, brittle, metallic in autumn), and then that the whole sequence is interpretable as the order in which the Five Powers generate each other throughout the year, would impress with a strong conviction of having perceived a true structural relationship.

The fitting of the Five Colours lacks this inevitability. None of them stands out as qualified for the central position, and the one established opposition ("white/black") was not, as one might think theoretically conceivable, seen as corresponding to "summer/winter." A calendrical scheme in *Guanzi* ch. 85, which links only the Four Seasons with four directions and four colours, fits "green/white" to "spring/autumn" (the contrast of vivid and paling leaves) and "yellow/black" to "summer/winter" (the contrast of sunshine and darkness). With the introduction of the Five

Powers into the scheme, the second pair is changed to "red/black," and yellow, as the colour of soil, is reserved for the middle position.

The tight scheme of the seasons, directions and Powers loosens in extending to the colours and beyond, but it interconnects remarkably with another sequence wholly independent of it, the conquest cycle of the Five Powers. Some at least of the successive conquests are considerably older than the earliest documentation of the generation cycle correlated with the seasons; the *Zuozhuan* in the 4th century BCE records prognostications based on the conquest of fire by water and of metal by fire.[34] Among Chinese protoscientific concepts, the conquest cycle stands out as independent of all correlations, and probably derives directly from observation of the five basic resources at the workman's disposal. Struggling with water, fire, metal, wood or soil, there is little room for disagreement as to which of the others is most required to dam, quench, melt, cut or dig the resisting material. Granted that fire as well as metal can conquer wood, one burns wood to get rid of it or to warm oneself, it is metal which is used to shape it to one's will. In noticing that there is a single and *different* answer in each case (at any rate before metal superseded wooden spade and plough), and that the conquests connect in an unbroken cycle, one would seem to have discovered in the courses of action specific to the basic materials a regularity on Earth comparable to the cycles observed in Heaven (cf. *Zuozhuan Zhao* 32/6 故天有三辰，地有五行 'Therefore Heaven has the Three *Chen* (sun, moon, stars), Earth has the Five Processes'). Why is it then, ancient Chinese and modern structuralist are alike compelled to ask, that when the two independent sequences are compared, it turns out that in the one required to correlate with seasons and directions, each Power is generating the immediate predecessor of the Power which it conquers?

Conquests : Fire Metal Wood Soil Water Fire

Generation : Fire Soil Metal Water Wood Fire Soil

To answer that the fitting of the Powers to seasons and directions must have been guided by this symmetry would be to overlook the structural restraints which allowed no other option except to fit "fire/water" implausibly to "spring/autumn" and "wood/metal" to "summer/winter." One can only suppose that the symmetry is an accidental effect of interposing soil among the pairs of opposites which have to be put together in the conquest order (since conquest implies opposition) but on facing sides of the square in the pattern correlating with the seasons and directions. The Chinese cosmologists themselves have a much neater explanation. Like scientists subsuming under a wider law of nature, they discover a larger structure which accounts for both sequences. *Huainanzi* ch. 4 postulates that each of the Five itself passes through five stages of rise and decline.[35]

Birth	Wood	Fire	Soil	Metal	Water
Prime	Water	/Wood	Fire	Soil	Metal
Aging	Metal	Water	/Wood	Fire	Soil
Immobilisation	Soil	Metal	Water	/Wood	Fire
Death	Fire	Soil	Metal	Water	/Wood

So at its prime each generates the one which is born and conquers the one which dies.

One's first impression that the correlations of Chinese proto-science are inherently loose and arbitrary requires some qualification. It has a structure which loosens as it expands, but with interrelations tight enough to impress a modern analyst as requiring explanation in his own terms, genetic explanation; he may see the system as growing and integrating under the influence of chance factors rather as an organism develops by incorporating chance mutations. (The looseness with which it has to be applied in accounting for phenomena is another matter). It is not that the conquest cycle as a series of relations is too vague for us to acknowledge it as significant – water does quench fire, which does melt metal – but that for us any cycle of physical relations between things selected and associated solely for their utility to mankind can only be accidental. From a modern viewpoint, Chinese proto-science can be discovering significant connections between phenomena only when there are indeed parallel causal relations between things contrasted as Yin and Yang, or there are causal relations with the seasons or the directions, the two strong correlates of the Five Powers. Where the system takes leave altogether of what nowadays we would recognise as fact, its fruitful possibilities will presumably be limited to the mathematical relations of numerology. Here we may consider a problem to which John Major has called attention.[36] The Five Powers in the generation order correlate, as we have seen, with the four cardinal points arranged as in a mandala around a centre.

            Fire

Wood   Soil   Metal

           Water

Suppose that we rearrange in the conquest order, and replace the names of the Powers by their numbers, with the Yin number of each pair (the completing, so even) after the Yang (the generating, so odd) in the direction chosen, thus filling in the intermediate points. This forms the diagram traditionally identified since the Song dynasty as the Luo Document (*Luo shu* 洛書) mentioned in the *Great Appendix* of the *Changes* (to be read anticlockwise, from soil through water).

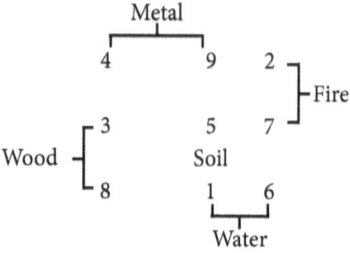

Why has this procedure resulted in a magic square, with the numbers adding up to 15 in every direction? Is it possible that the magic square was first discovered by this very operation? It is documented in China from the 1st century CE,[37] earlier than in any other civilisation,[38] and became a speciality of Chinese mathematics, which by the 13th century CE had developed magic squares to the order of 10. The alternative is to suppose that the numbers of the Five Powers were themselves taken from the magic square interpreted as a symbol of the conquest cycle. If so, the order of enumeration in the *Hongfan* is not arbitrary, and implies knowledge of the magic square some 500 years before its first documentation. Major, who is now convinced of its great antiquity, has shifted from the first to the second position.[39] It may seem that the first assumes a nearly incredible mathematical coincidence which the second eliminates. But this impression fades on closer examination. The Five Powers are a set of five each allotted a number and the number plus five. When the mandala-like grouping round a centre is extended from the cardinal to the intermediate points, we have a five surrounded by pairs of numbers separated by five, which is already the skeleton of a major square. A numerologist at work on it will be trying out every option looking for some fascinating symmetry. If he starts from a cardinal point putting Yang before Yin numbers, one of only six ways of arranging the pairs will lead him directly to the magic square. Does it still appear surprising that the result should coincide with the conquest order? But we had the choice of reading clockwise or anti-clockwise, and would have been equally impressed if it had turned out to be the generation order. Of the six arrangements, four will be readable either clockwise or anti-clockwise as either the generation or the conquest order. The agreement with the conquest order is therefore irrelevant; what matters is that the prospect of the magic square was latent from the start in the allotment of numbers to a group of five correlated with the cardinal points. Whether or not the discovery was made in this way – it is not a question to which one would expect a definitive answer – this well illustrates the theoretical possibility of speculation about the Five Powers leading to an important discovery. To the numerologist himself, of course, the agreement with the conquest order would seem highly relevant. One can imagine the joy and wonder of discovering that in the *observed* order in which the basic materials of Earth conquer each other (for anyone can see that fire melts metal, metal cuts wood and so on all the way round) each one at every stage is united to all the rest by changing numbers which always add up to the same. Better still, the outer four derive from soil at the centre through the two of Yin and Yang, through binary oppositions opening out from "Between/within"; the numbers on either side of five always add up to twice five. The discovery of the Inverse Square Law of gravitation itself would hardly have made a stronger impression of seeing right through to the mathematical secret of the cosmos.

Another line of thought springing from contemplation of this mandala fitted to the cardinal points is traced by Needham in v.4/1 of *Science and civilisation in China*. The importance of placing oneself in relation to the cosmic influence inspired an exploration of the South-pointing property of the lodestone and then of magnetised iron. The principle of needle and dial, so fecund for technology, is the discovery of diviners and geomancers, whose compass has the needle pointing to the Five Phases and Eight Trigrams as well as the cardinal points. The invention and development of the compass, however, in having to survive the practical testing of effects, brings us down to the realm of causal thinking, irrelevant to the present study. Causal thinking would have to be the main factor in the fertility in invention of China (exceeding, on Needham's estimate, that of pre-modern Europe), whatever the interconnections with what passed for science. We have insisted throughout that the organising of proto-sciences by correlation within a society's patterning of concepts has nothing to do with the extent to which the concepts are being used for causal explanation and practical invention. The only technology proper to correlative system-building itself is magic. This was still true of Renaissance Europe; Kepler earned his living as a court astrologer, Giordano Bruno the great defender of the Copernican hypothesis turns out under the scrutiny of Frances Yates to have been primarily a master of the hermetic and cabbalistic arts. It remains of course true today – the occultism, seemingly moribund, which revived in the 19th century with the *Transcendental magic* of Éliphas Lévi, the 20th-century revival of astrology, the importation with Jung's blessing of Chinese divination into the West. One has only to re-examine the "Therefores" we italicised in the *Huainanzi* cosmogony to see that if such methods can explain or predict anything, they can predict the outcome of wars, the death of kings, whether the lonely girl will meet a dark handsome man next week.

We have so far been treating pre-Galilean cosmologies with some condescension as mere proto-science, the superseded predecessors of Newtonian physics. But a cosmos of the old kind has also an advantage to which post-Galilean science makes no claim; those who live in it know not only what is but what should be. To correlate does not detach one from the spontaneous assimilations and differentiations which precede analysis, in which expecting the same as before one is already responding in favour of it or against, as illustrated above by the case of Pavlov's dog; in anticipating what will happen one knows how to act. The objectivised world of modern science dissolves this primitive synthesis of fact and value, and in facilitating successful explanation and prediction leaves us to find our values elsewhere. Many are unhappy to be thus exiled from the sources of value; Westerners today who toss coins to read the hexagrams seem actually to feel more at home in the traditional cosmos of China. There man still stands at the centre of things in interaction with the rest, and has only to contrast A with B to respond to them as superior and inferior, better and worse.

Seen from this direction as a scheme relating man to community and cosmos, a correlative world-view discloses a much more favourable aspect. The primary social institution, language, is the one for which we judged correlative thinking perfectly adequate. Institutions in general require that for most of the time we adjust to pattern automatically, analysing only when faced with an occasion for considered choice. Politics, sociology and psychology have never attained that detachment from correlative thinking which, on the analogy of physics, should be required by their claim to be "sciences." Among the shapers of contemporary social and political thought, an especially striking example is the visionary who shares with Robert Owen the distinction of being pre-Marxian founder of socialism, Charles Fourier, a fantast of the calibre of Zou Yan himself. His Utopia, which displays his genius for imagining individuals with idiosyncratic needs and talents in combinations which would allow their disparate natural inclinations to work out to their mutual benefit, was only part of an extraordinary cosmology partially suppressed by his embarrassed disciples (to take the most notorious example, he expected that at the appropriate phase of the cosmic cycle the sea would turn into lemonade). Apart from all theories, much of ordinary practical life belongs irredeemably to correlative thinking. To our previous observations about correlative thinking in the arts, exemplified by *Heart of darkness*, we may add that any correlative system is poetically stimulating to those in sympathy with it, a treasury of metaphor and metonym. The thinking which relates "white/black" to "west/north," "autumn/winter," "metal/water" no longer looks silly when it relates them to "weddings/funerals," nor is one embarrassed that the Chinese choose white for funerals and the West black. Even the scientific pretensions look better from the social perspective. They provide a solution to the universal problem of how to act in ignorance. When information is inadequate, it is better to decide by a diviner's prediction than not to decide at all, not to mention that a suitably opaque prognostication may stimulate rather than exempt from thought and decision.

In tabulating correlations of fives we did not explain their function in the source used, the calendrical chapters of the *Lüshi chunqiu*. We repeat the major correlations:

	A	B	Between	C	D
(Five Powers)	Wood	Fire	Soil	Metal	Water
(Four Seasons)	Spring	Summer	—	Autumn	Winter
(Four Directions)	East	South	(Centre)	West	North
(Five Colours)	Green	Red	Yellow	White	Black

Throughout the year the Yang *qi* waxes at the expense of the Yin up to the solstice in the 5th month (mid-summer) and then wanes in favour of the Yin up to the solstice in the 11th month (mid-winter). With each season the Grand Historiographer announces the rise of the appropriate Power, robes are changed to the appropriate colour, and the ruler occupies the appropriate quarter of the palace, from East to South to West to North, moving from month to month through the three rooms of a quarter. Thus at the beginning of the year, when 'the east wind melts the ice and the hibernating insects stir' (東風解凍、蟄蟲始振) the Historiographer reports 'Such-and-such a day is the start of spring: the fullness of Power is in Wood' (某日立春,盛德在木). The ruler, wearing green, then leads out his nobles to welcome spring in the East suburb, rewards civil officials, issues orders to be merciful and bountiful to the people, pushes the plough three times to encourage farming, and commands the superintendent of agriculture to take up residence in the East suburb. Correspondingly, when 'the chill winds come, the white dew falls and the cold cicada chirps' (涼風至，白露降，寒蟬鳴) the Historiographer reports 'Such-and-such a day is the start of autumn: the fullness of Power is in Metal.' The ruler, wearing white, leads out the nobles to welcome autumn in the West suburb, rewards this time his military officials, and issues orders to become versed in the laws, repair the prisons and punish crime. Each month of the calendar ends with a warning against neglect of the prescribed ritual and practical measures.

Lüshi chunqiu (ch. 1/1) Xu 1/5B
孟春行夏令，則風雨不時，草木早槁，國乃有恐。行秋令，則民大疫，疾風暴雨數至，藜莠蓬蒿並興。行冬令，則水潦為敗，霜雪大摯，首種不入。

'If in the first spring month you enact the orders for summer, wind and rain will be untimely, grass and trees will wither early, the state will suffer alarms. If you enact the orders for autumn, the people will suffer plagues, whirlwinds and rainstorms will come frequently, brambles and weeds will spring up densely. If you enact the orders for winter, there will be damage from floods and disaster from snow and frost, and the first sowing will not take root.'

With the conduct of the ruler through the Four Seasons, we may compare the regime throughout the year recommended as healthy in ch. 2 of the medical classic *Huangdi neijing* 黃帝內經 ("Inner classic of the Yellow Emperor"), uncertainly dated but not far from the same period. The ruler imitates Heaven by being generous in spring and punishing in autumn; the healthy man helps the *qi* of the body (the vital forces nourished by the *qi* which are influences in the atmosphere) to revive in the kindness of spring and survive the punishments of autumn.

Both accounts conclude each sequence by recording the consequences of behaviour inappropriate to the season. In both, correlation with the seasons presents the problem of having to omit the middle member of the five, which in the case of the Five Viscera (*Wu zang* 五臟) is the spleen. The royal calendar in *Guanzi* ch. 85 even shares with the medical classic a formula for behaving indulgently in spring: 'Let them live, don't kill them; reward them, don't punish them' (生而勿殺，賞而勿罰).[40]

	A	B	C	D
1.	Spring	Summer	Autumn	Winter
2.	Coming to life	Growing up	Gathering in	Storing away
3.	Liver	Heart	Lungs	Kidneys

Position 2 transfers metaphorically (not of course within the same scheme) from the crops to the *qi* of the body.

Huangdi neijing (ch. 2) SBCK 1/11A–13A

春三月，此謂發陳。天地俱生，萬物以榮，夜臥早起，廣步於庭，被髮緩形，以使志生，生而勿殺，予而勿奪，賞而勿罰。此春氣之應，養生之道也。逆之則傷肝，夏爲寒變，奉長者少。夏三月，此謂蕃秀。天地氣交，萬物華實，夜臥早起，無厭於日，使志無怒，使華英成秀，使氣得泄，若所愛在外。此夏氣之應，養長之道也。逆之則傷心，秋爲痎瘧，奉收者少，冬至重病。秋三月，此謂容平。天氣以急，地氣以明，早臥早起，與雞俱興，使志安寧，以緩秋刑，收斂神氣，使秋氣平，無外其志，使肺氣清。此秋氣之應，養收之道也。逆之則傷肺，冬爲飧泄，奉藏者少。冬三月，此謂閉藏。水冰地坼，無擾乎陽，早臥晚起，必待日光，使志若伏若匿，若有私意，若已有得，去寒就溫，無泄皮膚，使氣亟奪。此冬氣之應，養藏之道也。逆之則傷腎，春爲痿厥，奉生者少。

'The three months of spring one calls "the issuing and laying out."
Together Heaven and Earth give life,
The myriad creatures thereby blossom.
Sleep at night and rise early,
Stroll at ease around the yard,
Loose the hair, relax the body,
Allow intent to come to life.
Let it live, don't kill it:
Give to it, don't steal from it:
Reward it, don't punish it.

This is the response to the *qi* of spring, the way to nourish the coming to life. If you go against it you harm the liver and in summer will suffer from chills; there will be too little provision for the growing up.

'The three months of summer one calls "the thriving and fulfilment."
The *qi* of Heaven and Earth mingle,
The myriad creatures flower and ripen.
Sleep at night and rise early,
Don't be too greedy for the sunshine,
Don't let intent get out of hand,
Let flowering fulfil its growth,
Allow the *qi* to seep out from you,
As though the not-to-be-wasted were outside.

This is the response to the *qi* of summer, the way to nourish the growing up. If you go against it you harm the heart and in autumn will suffer from fevers; there will be too little provision for the gathering in. (*Gloss?* 'And grave illness at the winter solstice')

'The three months of autumn one calls
"the contained and calm."
The *qi* of Heaven is then gusty,
The *qi* of Earth is then bright.
Sleep early, rise early,
Be up with the cock.
Keep intents firm and stable,
To ease the penalties of autumn.
Gather in the harvest of daemonic *qi*
Keep the *qi* of autumn calm.
Don't let intent stray outside,
Keep the *qi* in the lungs clear.

This is the response to the *qi* of autumn, the way to nourish the gathering in. If you go against it you harm the lungs and in winter will suffer from diarrhoea; there will be too little provision for the storing away.

'The three months of winter one calls "the shutting up and storing away."
Water freezes, ground cracks,
Don't put strain on the Yang.
Sleep early, rise late,

Be sure to wait for the sunshine.
Keep an intent as though lurking, hiding.
As though it were a private thought,
As though you had succeeded already.
Avoid the cold, stay near the warm,
Don't allow the seeping through the skin
Which lets the *qi* be quickly stolen away.

This is the response to the *qi* of winter, the way to nourish the storing away. If you go against it you harm the kidneys and in spring will suffer from impotence; there will be too little provision for the giving of life.'

Both the royal calendars and the medical regime place us in a world which is not, like that of post-Galilean science, bound by invariable law. The interactions of things are seen as either orderly or chaotic; they are orderly to the extent that in the symmetries of space and cycles of time the harmonious are together and the conflicting apart. To describe a phenomenon in its place and time within this order will be to select from the conflicting (as paradigmatic A, B ...) and to combine the harmonious (as syntagmatic 1, 2 ...). This cosmology differs also from modern science in that man's action belongs within the total interaction, supporting or disturbing the order. That it is inside the interaction is especially plain in the medical account, where the *qi* of the body is responding through the seasons to the *qi* of the atmosphere; even the *zhi* 志 "intent," which is the Chinese concept closest to our "will," is far from being a Kantian will detached from spontaneous inclination, it is impulse roused by spring and stabilised by autumn. In the sense that a regular recurrence exciting an impulse to corresponding movement is called a "rhythm," the cycle of the seasons is not merely a recurrence usable for prediction but a rhythm with which man, like other creatures, stays in step. When the ruler issues largesse in spring and punishes in autumn, it is not at all that he has inferred how to act from a set of artificial analogies and a dubious jump from "is" to "ought"; he is spontaneously moved to generosity by the kindly breath of spring and to just wrath by the breath of autumn which kills the leaves when their time has come. To interfere with the natural rhythm which inclines him to benignity in spring and severity in autumn would damage his own capacity to reconcile the conflicting demands of benevolence and duty. Nor is there anything artificial in his wearing green in spring and white in autumn; they are the colours which in Chinese custom will put him in the mood to respond fully to the seasons, as in Western culture the spirit in which a couple enter marriage might be considerably affected by the bride wearing black.

In this cosmos it is hard to recognise the line we are accustomed to draw between fact, which belongs to science, and value, which is outside it. Is the line genuinely absent or merely obscured? Let us try to draw it, taking as example the proportional opposition "spring : bounty :: autumn : punishment."

Paradigm Spring compares with autumn as bounty with punishment.

Syntagm Spring connects with bounty as autumn with punishment.

> How does Heaven act in the two seasons?

Heaven generates life in spring and kills it off in autumn.

> How ought the ruler act?

The ruler ought to be bountiful in spring and punish in autumn.

> How ought one to take care of one's health?

One ought to indulge the body in spring and restrain it in autumn.

Shall we conclude then that Chinese cosmological thinking, among its other weaknesses, confuses fact and value? But that word "ought," which has no equivalent in the Chinese texts (although they do use the negative imperatives, *wu* 無 （=母） *wu* 勿), seems not quite apt; the texts tell us not what man ought to do but what he is stimulated to do when the cosmic interactions are orderly. Shall we look for the "ought" further back, in the obligation to take the measures which maintain rather than disturb the order? But in the medical example one is not taking the measures good for one's health because one judges order better than disorder; they are the measures one is moved to take when one understands how the seasons act on the body. Similarly the actions prescribed for the ruler are the actions to which he is spontaneously moved, within the interactions of Heaven and Earth, if he understands how things compare and connect. Man is in spontaneous interaction with things, but responds differently according to the degree of his understanding of their similarities and contrasts, connection or isolation. The "ought" then finally detaches itself in an imperative to know how things compare and connect, and in particular whether in connecting they support or interfere with each other, which is to know their "patterns" (*li* 理)

and the "Way" (*Dao* 道) behind them all; to know what to do is to know what one would be moved to do in the sage's full knowledge of how things are related in fact. Value separates from fact as the value of wisdom itself. One might find the same relation of fact and value in the correlative thinking of an artist, as in Conrad's story analysed earlier. Since the reader's spontaneous prejudices and impulses to action change with his understanding of how things are related in fact, to judge the effect good assumes only that if the understanding is deepened the change is for the better.

The philosophical problem of "is" and "ought" is of course too complicated for detailed discussion here. My own position, defended in detail elsewhere, is that this way of relating awareness and spontaneity is characteristic of Chinese philosophy in general and that it offers a genuine solution of the problem.[41] If so, Chinese cosmology has the logical advantage, not indeed over post-Galilean science (which is not concerned with "ought"), but over the kind of "scientism" which tries to ground value in biological, sociological or psychological facts. It would even follow that it is only in the fields where correlative thinking still reigns, in practical life and in the arts, that modern man isolated from cosmos is not either confusing fact and value or else assuming values groundlessly. But whatever position is taken on this question, the Chinese system of correlations looks altogether more solid in its social than in its scientific application. Wearing the wrong colour or standing at the wrong cardinal point will not act causally on the seasons and disrupt the natural order, but within Chinese society they will indeed act causally on the ruler's capacity to perform his seasonal duties.

5
BINARY STRUCTURE:
THE CHANGES

On the vast system of the *Book of Changes* we have only one observation to make. The evolution of binary oppositions (with the possibility of the "Between" supervening at any stage) has a numerical structure which seems that of the cosmos itself until habituation to exact observation and measurement leads to the exposure of a quite different structure by mathematised science. Among the classical philosophers, with their cosmos abbreviated to Heaven and Earth proceeding along the Way through the Four Seasons, the author of *Laozi* has a glimpse of it:

Laozi 42
道生一，一生二，二生三，三生萬物

'The Way generates the One, the One generates the two, the two generate three, the three generate the myriad creatures.'

The "Great music" chapter of the *Lüshi chunqiu* has a fuller account.

Lüshi chunqiu (ch. 5) Xu 5/4B-5A
音樂之所由來者遠矣。生於度量，本於太一。太一出兩儀，兩儀出陰陽。陰陽變化……四時代興，或署或寒，或短或長，或柔或剛。萬物所出，造於太一，化於陰陽。

'The source from which music comes is far back. It is born from measure, rooted in the Supreme One. The Supreme One emits the Two Exemplars, the Two Exemplars emit the Yin and Yang. The Yin and Yang alter and transform …. The Four Seasons arise in turn, now hot now cold, now short now long, now soft now hard. At the source from which the myriad creatures issue, they are set going by the Supreme One, are transformed by the Yin and Yang.'

One reason for the fascination exerted by the *Changes* since this old manual of divination entered philosophy towards the end of the 3rd century BCE is that it provides a perfect symbolism for the numerical skeleton of the evolving cosmos. The building upwards of the hexagrams line by line with two choices for each line corresponds precisely to the structure conceived to organise the phenomena they are used to predict.

Great Appendix II (*Zhou Yi* HY *Xi* A, 11)
是故易有太極，是生兩儀。兩儀生四像，四象生八卦，八卦定吉凶。

'Therefore in the Changes there is the Supreme Pole. This generates the Two Exemplars, the Two Exemplars generate the Four Images, the Four Images generate the Eight Trigrams. The Eight Trigrams fix the auspicious and the baleful.'

The two alternatives at the first step are the "exemplars" of all pairs (Heaven and Earth, Yin and Yang, …), the four at the second step are the "images" of all fours (Four Seasons, Four Directions, …), the eight at the third step are the trigrams, and so on up to the 64 hexagrams. The trigrams have a wide range of symbolism expounded in the appendix "Explanation of the Trigrams" (*Shuo gua* 說卦), but represent primarily the four pairs Heaven/Earth, mountain/marsh, water/fire, thunder/wind. This symbolism, attested in the *Zuozhuan* as already current among diviners by the 4th century BCE,[42] is independent of the correlations of the Five Phases, which are not mentioned in the appendices. The Eight Trigrams and Five Phases do however share the pair water/fire, and also their correlation with North/South.

Eight Trigrams

Kun	Gen	Kan	Xun	Zhen	Li	Dui	Qian
坤	艮	坎	巽	震	離	兌	乾
Earth	Mountains	Water	Wind	Thunder	Fire	Marshes	Heaven
☷	☶	☵	☴	☳	☲	☱	☰

Four Images

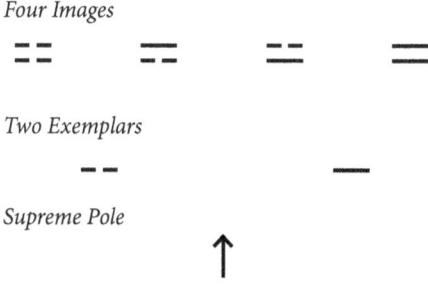

Two Exemplars

Supreme Pole

Continuing to build upwards stage by stage, one arrives at the 64 hexagrams in the *Xiantian* 先天 "Ahead of Heaven" order first attested in the *Huangji jingshi shu* 皇極經世書 of Shao Yong 邵雍 (1011–1077). For a modern reader, the perfection of the diagrams as symbols of binary unfolding is well illustrated by the fact that if he substitutes the figures 0 and 1 for the broken and unbroken lines he can at each level read off the binary numerals counting from 0.

Two Exemplars: 0, 1.
Four Images: 00, 01, 10, 11 (Decimal numerals 0 to 3)
Eight Trigrams: 000, 001, 010, 011, 100, 101, 110, 111
    (Decimal numerals 0 to 7).

The completed hexagrams in sequence then read as the binary numerals from 0 to 63. This substitution has nothing to do with Chinese thought, for which the number ascribed to the unbroken or Yang line is 1 and to the broken or Yin line 2. But it has attracted the attention of Westerners ever since Leibnitz, who noticed the correspondence almost immediately after he had established the foundations of binary arithmetic.[43] Now that the digital computer has come to be accepted as a fruitful model for understanding the workings of the brain, we may recognise the *Xiantian* order as an important discovery to which correlative thinking was entirely appropriate. The Chinese tracing a symmetry from figure to figure were looking into what seemed to them to be the structure of the cosmos itself. If by "cosmos" one understands the universe as ordered by the mind, they were not altogether wrong. They had discovered the structure, or as much of it as is binary, in the primary ordering of the similar and the different which establishes the outline for science to fill in, the pattern in the unfolding of 'the first of the metaphysical oppositions, that between the same and the other', which for Kepler was still not the start but the end of cosmology. To say the same in other words, this system unfolding from an origin unsymbolisable within the system is the most precise formulation Chinese thought ever achieved of what it understood by the "Way."

APPENDIX:
THE EARLY HISTORY OF YIN-YANG AND THE FIVE PHASES

An implication of this structuralist analysis is that one should not think of Chinese correlative thinking as the application of the metaphysical theories about Yin and Yang and the Five Phases. It leads us to expect that diachronically concepts would organise in groups which in the process of being correlated would tend to segregate along the axis 1, 2, 4 …, with or without an extra member for the position "Between/within." Only as the system takes shape would the need arise to find principles which unite as similar and distinguish as different. In ancient China such a principle is a specific *qi*, an influence from the atmosphere or within the body, which for example, once spring is correlated with the colour green and the ruler's bounty, will be conceived as changing the weather to spring, making leaves green and moving the heart to bounty. Here we shall merely sketch the history from this angle, making few additions to the classic account by Xu Fuguan.

Down to the 4th century BCE, as Xu Fuguan shows, *yang* and *yin* were current words for "sunshine" and "shade," in particular for the sunny and shady sides of mountain and river. Thus in the core chapters of *Mozi* (ch. 8–37) the pair is found only in the sentence 'This is why the heat and cold made by Heaven are in proportion, the Four Seasons are in tune, sunshine, shade, rain and dew are timely' (*Mozi* HY 27/30 是以天之爲寒熱也節，四時調，陰陽雨露也時。) In the cosmology of the *Zuozhuan* and *Guoyu*, which still shows no clear tendency to group in twos and fives, sunshine and shade are classed among the "Six *Qi*" of Heaven.[44] The physician He 和, diagnosing the Marquis of Jin's 晉 illness as the effect of sexual excesses and incurable, provides the fullest illustration.

Zuozhuan Duke Zhao 1/*fu* 8

天有六氣,降生五味,發爲五色,徵爲五聲,淫生六疾。六氣曰陰陽,風雨,晦明也。分爲四時,序爲五節,過則爲菑。陰淫寒疾,陽淫熱疾,風淫末疾,雨淫腹疾,晦淫惑疾,明淫心疾。女陽物而晦時,淫則生內熱惑之疾。

'Heaven has the Six *Qi*, which descending generate the Five Tastes, issue as the Five Colours, are evidenced by the Five Sounds, and in excess generate the Six Diseases. The Six *Qi* are shade and sunshine, wind and rain, dark and light. They divide to make the Four Seasons, in sequence make the Five Rhythms, and in excess bring about calamity. From shade in excess cold diseases, from sunshine hot; from wind in excess diseases of the extremities, from rain of the stomach; from dark in excess delusions, from light diseases of the heart. Woman being a thing of the sunshine but of the dark time, in excess she generates the diseases of inward heat and deluding poisons.'

Here the tastes, colours and sounds correlate not with the Five Phases but with the Six *Qi*. Sunshine and shade are associated primarily not with light and dark (a separate pair) but with heat and cold, as may be noticed throughout the *Zuozhuan*. Woman, who in the later system is very definitely not Yang but Yin, belongs with the warmth of sunshine.

Outside cosmology, the word *qi* is used primarily, as it had been since the *Analects*, of the breath and other energies of the body, frequently paired with the blood (*xueqi* 血氣 "blood and *qi*"), or of temperament, for example martial spirit (*yongqi* 勇氣). But early Chinese psychology is outward-looking, conceiving the forces of the body as entering it from outside.

Guoyu (ch. 3) 125
口內味而耳內聲，聲味生氣。氣在口爲言，在目爲明.

'The mouth draws in tastes and the ear sounds, sounds and tastes generate *qi*, the *qi* in the mouth become speech, in the eye become sight.'

Zuozhuan Zhao 9/*fu* 2
味以行氣，氣以實志，志以定言。

'By tastes one guides the *qi* (by food energises the body), by the *qi* makes intent solid, by intent fixes speech.'

Zhi 志 "intent, inclination" itself springs from the atmospheric influences, as in the *Huangdi neijing*.[45]

Zuozhuan Zhao 25 summer
民有好惡喜怒哀樂生于六氣。是故審則宜類，以制六志。

'The likes and dislikes of the people, being pleased with or angry, sorrow and joy, are generated from the Six *Qi*. Therefore take care to model yourself on the appropriate categories (correlate dress, food, music) in order to control the Six Inclinations.'

The *Jie* 戒 chapter of *Guanzi*[46] lists the same six inclinations as themselves the Six *Qi*. This reflects the tendency to turn attention inwards towards the heart (*xin* 心) noticeable also in *Mencius* and *Zhuangzi*. The *Inner chapters* of *Zhuangzi* likewise refer to the Six *Qi* and, in the manner of *Zuozhuan* medicine, to the 'inward heat' (*neire* 內熱) of a man making himself ill by worry as 'a yin-yang affliction' (*yinyang zhi huan* 陰陽之患).[47] A difference is that Zhuangzi uses *yin* and *yang* not of atmospheric influences but of the *qi* in the body which warm and chill and which when discordant bring it to sickness and death.[48] In this internalisation of sunshine and shade the pair is already detached from wind and rain, light and dark. Since the "nurture of life" (*yangsheng* 養生) was a concern shared by medicine and Taoist meditation, Zhuangzi may be borrowing from the terminology of medicine. At what stage did the pair emerge as the principles behind all cosmic oppositions? The test is whether they are correlated with cosmic pairs, in particular with "Heaven/Earth," as in this passage of the 3rd or 2nd century BCE from the *Mixed chapters*:

> *Zhuangzi* HY 25/67, 69
> 是故天地者形之大者也，陰陽者氣之大者也。……萬物之所生惡起。大公調曰，陰陽相照相蓋相治，四時相代相生相殺。

> 'Therefore Heaven and Earth are the greatest of shapes, Yin and Yang the greatest of *qi* …. "Whence did it arise, that from which the myriad creatures were born?" Dagong Diao said: "Yin and Yang illuminate, hide and regulate each other; the Four Seasons succeed, generate and execute each other …."'

There is no evidence of Yin-Yang dualism confidently datable as earlier than Zou Yan, who is described by Sima Qian as writing some 100,000 words about 'the growth and diminution of Yin and Yang' (*yinyang xiaoxi* 陰陽消息).[49] It is not, however, likely to be his invention; it is too deeply rooted, not only in the *Lüshi chunqiu* but in the *Outer* and *Mixed chapters* of *Zhuangzi* and in *Xunzi*, neither of which shows any interest in systematised correspondences. Given the prominence of binary oppositions in all traditional Chinese thought, the choice of Yin and Yang as the *qi* from which they start would be a natural step once the pair had been isolated as the two *qi* in the body. Light and dark would be easily discarded from the Six *Qi* as implicit in sunshine and shade; even the *Zuozhuan* drops them in correlating rain, sunshine, wind and shade with the Four Seasons.[50] The final step, with Yang and Yin at the head of a chain including *qing* 清 "clear"/*zhuo* 濁 "muddy," is the *Huainanzi* cosmogony in which the whole universe forms by the clear *qi* rising to become Heaven and the muddy sinking to become Earth.

Turning now to sets of fours and fives, the question which concerns us is how the *qi* behind them came to be identified as the *Wu xing*, for which the accepted translation was formerly "Five Elements" but is now "Five Phases."[51] The new translation, although appropriate from the Han onwards, exposes us to a new danger, of assuming that the *Wu xing* were from the first stages in cosmic cycles. Even the habit of thinking of wood, fire and the rest of them as having always been called the *Wu xing* tends to obscure two important facts about their early history.

(1) In pre-Han thought the set wood, fire, soil, metal and water has different aspects called by different names. The old cosmology of the *Zuozhuan* uses not only *Wu xing* but *wu cai* 五材 "Five Materials" and *liu fu* 六府 "Six Storehouses" (the five with the addition of grain).[52] When we come to the crucial thinker and crucial document in the emergence of the later cosmology, the term *Wu xing* actually disappears temporarily from sight. Zou Yan, as reported by Sima Qian, speaks consistently of the *wu de* 五德 "Five Powers"[53]; the *Lüshi chunqiu* mentions only the *de* and the *qi*.[54] There are important distinctions here which later usage confused.

(2) Classifications of moral conduct often make such groupings as *wu cai*[55] "Five Talents," *wu de*[56] "Five Virtues" and *wu xing* "five courses of action." There are examples

of the last, the items different in each case, in *Xunzi* HY 20/48, *Lüshi chunqiu* (ch. 14/1) Xu 14/2B/1, *Huainanzi* (ch. 15) Liu 15/19B. The most interesting is in a document, Mencian in tendency, attached to Mawangdui manuscript A of *Laozi*. Here the *wu xing* are benevolence, duty, manners, wisdom and sagehood, a series found also in *Mencius* 7B/24. This has finally resolved an old puzzle, the baffling reference to Mencius as teaching the *wu xing* in *Xunzi* 6/11. Although these usages have nothing directly to do with the *Wu xing* of cosmology, they strongly suggest that the five *cai*, *de* and *xing* are related as *cai* 才 "the stuff one is made of," *de* "power, virtue" and *xing* "conduct" are related in a person. The Mawangdui manuscript begins with six parallel sentences about the five courses of action; we select from the unmutilated the one about manners.

Laozi Jia ben juan hou guyi shu 老子甲本卷后古佚書2A
禮刑（＝形）於内胃（＝謂）之德之行，
不刑於内胃之行。

'If manners have taken shape within, one calls it "the enactment of the power"; if they have not taken shape within, one calls it "the action."'

With this may be compared a comment by Pei Yin 裴駰 of the Liu Song 劉宋 dynasty (CE 420–478) on a reference to Zou Yan by Sima Qian:

Shiji jijie 史記集解 (Ch. 28) 1369 n. 3
如淳曰，今其書有五德終始。五德各以所勝爲行。秦謂周爲火德，滅火者水，故自謂水德。

'Ruchun says: "There is at present an "Ends and starts of the Five Powers" in his book. Each of the Five Powers is *enacted* by the conquest of another. Qin ascribed to Zhou the Power of Fire; the extinguisher of fire is water, so it ascribed to itself the Power of Water."'

One is accustomed to ask the question "Why would wood or metal be called a *xing* 'going'?," and seek an answer in terms of Han and later concepts of them as *qi* passing through the phases of a cycle. But it looks as though this is just another of the pseudo-problems in which a sinologist again and again finds himself trapped by later uses of words. Down to 300 BCE, as Xu Fuguan perceived, water, fire and the rest of them are the resources provided by Earth for human labour, explicitly called *cai* 材 "materials" and included with grain among the *fu* 府 "storehouses." They are not *qi* at all (it is sunshine, shade, wind, rain, dark and light, influences from Heaven, which are *qi*). In the conquest cycle, it is the process (*xing* 行) specific to water, its wetting and going down, which conquers the flaming and rising of fire. When, about 250 BCE, Zou Yan applies the cycle to dynasties, he has to detach from fire the power or virtue which makes it flame and rise, and claim that it activated the Zhou, was nourished by their institutions, and in due course will be overcome by the power or virtue of water activating a new dynasty. Only these powers abstracted from the materials are yet conceivable as belonging to *qi*. The distinctions between materials, powers and processes are observed right down to *Huainanzi*,[57] and it is only after they lapse that the *Wu xing* as cyclic episodes in the evolutions of the universal *qi* are aptly represented in English by the "Five Phases."

This proposal is not inconsistent with the classic account of the *Wu xing* as the first of nine sets listed as essential to government in the "Grand Scheme" (*Hongfan* 洪範), one of the latest of the *Documents*, from perhaps about 400 BCE if one accepts it as earlier than the *Zuozhuan*.[58]

一、五行。一曰水，二曰火，三曰木，四曰金，五曰土。水曰潤下，火曰炎上，木曰曲直，金曰從革，土爰稼穡。……
二、五事。一曰貌，二曰言，三曰視，四曰聽，五曰思。貌曰恭，言曰從，視曰明，聽曰聰，思曰睿。

'1. The five processes. 1, water: 2, fire: 3, wood: 4, metal: 5, soil. Water: wetting, sinking. Fire: flaming, rising. Wood: bending,

straight. Metal: assuming the form imposed. In soil one plants and harvests. …
2. The five things to do. 1, demeanour: 2, speech: 3, looking: 4, listening: 5, thinking. Demeanour: respectful. Speech: in accord. Looking: seeing clearly. Listening: hearing clearly. Thinking: understanding.'

In the second series it is plain that the "thing to do" (*shi* 事) is not the demeanour, nor the respect, but assuming a respectful demeanour. The concept is split into its two components, loosely linked by using the particle *yue* 曰. Similarly the *xing* is not the water, nor wetting or sinking in general, but water wetting or sinking. The *xing* should then be the processes specific to each material, of which the workman takes advantage when he waters ground, sets alight from below, carpenters according to the grain of the wood, casts metal, plants grain.

The five natural processes most useful to man stand at the head of the nine sets of the Grand Scheme, the five actions required of man stand next. The operations of the materials basic to the people's livelihood are thus seen as the foundation of ordered society. Consequently the misgovernment by Gun 鯀 which preceded the revelation of the Grand Scheme is described as his disordering of the *Wu xing*, as also is the misgovernment of Youhu 有扈氏 in another of the Documents, the *Kanshi* 甘誓.[59] Both references may be understood in the light of a long account of rulers' extravagance in *Huainanzi* ch. 8, which runs through the wasteful uses of the five materials in turn.[60] The central importance of the *Wu xing* is shown also by the sacrifices to their five gods on the state altars of the land and the grain, of which we read in the *Zuozhuan*.[61] It may be presumed that these gods, rather than being the divinised materials, were the numinous agents behind the processes which make them useful; "the director of water" (*shuizheng* 水正) would ensure that water continues to wet and to sink, the "director of fire" (*huozheng* 火正) that fire continues to flame and to rise.

Xu Fuguan has shown convincingly that in the cosmology of the *Zuozhuan* and *Guoyu* the Five Materials and Five Processes are seen primarily as the resources put by Earth at man's disposal. But the conquest of metal by fire and fire by water were already being used in divination,[62] and it seems unnecessary to follow him in denying that the conquest cycle already existed. What may be safely denied is that they were the prime correlates of the colours, sounds and tastes, or that they were yet conceived as *qi*, which in this system are still the atmospheric influences from Heaven. It may be conceded that there would be some correlation with other fives, in divination and in the sacrifices to the gods in charge of the Five Processes. The order in which they are given in the *Zuozhuan* account of these gods[63] (wood, fire, metal, water, soil), together with the numbers by which they are listed in the *Hongfan*, rather suggests co-ordination with the cardinal points, grouped around the centre as in the later cosmology:

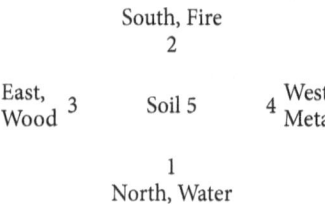

This arrangement is independent of the conquest cycle, but would not imply motion in the generation cycle until correlation was extended to the Four Seasons. A passage in the *Hongfan* fits the Five Processes to the Five Tastes, which would be decisive evidence of early correlation if it were not for a strong suspicion that it is an interpolation; it seems irrelevant to the context and is conspicuously ignored in the early Han *Shangshu dazhuan* 尚書大傳.[64] But whether or not such correlations began early, it is plain that in the *Zuozhuan* cosmology the prime correlates of colours, sounds and tastes were the Six *Qi* of Heaven, not the five Processes of Earth.

Zuozhuan Duke Zhao 25/2
夫禮。天之經也，地之義也，民之行也。天地之經而民實則之。則天之明，因地之性，生其六氣，用其五行。氣爲五味，發爲五色，章爲五聲。

'Ritual is the standard of Heaven, the exemplar of Earth, what the people perform. It is Heaven and Earth one has as standard, it is the people who take it as model. With the light of Heaven as model and the generativeness of Earth as basis, we generate their Six *Qi* and utilise their Five Processes. The *qi* become the Five Tastes, issue as the Five Colours, are proclaimed as the Five Sounds.'

The conquest cycle used in divination assumed tremendous political importance when Zou Yan applied it to the rise and fall of dynasties. The one full account of the doctrine (although not naming Zou Yan) is in the *Lüshi chunqiu*.

Lüshi chunqiu (ch. 13/2) Xu 13/7A
凡帝王者之將興也，天必先見祥乎下民。黃帝之時，天先見大螾大螻，黃帝曰：「土氣勝」土氣勝、故其色尚黃，其事則土。

'Whenever emperor or king is about to arise, Heaven is sure to display a good omen beforehand to the people below. In the time of the Yellow Emperor, Heaven displayed beforehand big earthworms and big ants [creatures of the soil]. The Yellow Emperor said: "The *qi* of Soil has conquered." Because the *qi* of Soil had conquered, as his colour he honoured yellow, for his affairs took Soil as model.'

The dynasties proceed as each *qi* is conquered by the next.

A	B	C	D	E
Yellow Emperor	Xia	Shang	Zhou	(Coming dynasty)
Soil	Wood	Metal	Fire	Water
Yellow	Green	White	Red	Black

Two points attract attention. The Five Powers are now correlated with the colours; and since the coming emperor will identify himself by the ritual acts which take Water as model, the more ritually usable correlations there are the better. The conditions are fulfilled for promoting them as the prime correlates of fours and fives, and therefore for elevating as an alternative to the conquest cycle a generation cycle running parallel with the

Four Seasons. Secondly, Zou Yan's abstraction of the Powers from the processes of the materials allows them to be treated as *qi* like the Yin and Yang, energising fluids which unify the similar and distinguish the different in chains of oppositions. In this passage the *Lüshi chunqiu* does refer to them as *qi*.

On this analysis the motivation for correlation with the Five Powers was basically political. Their substitution for the Four Seasons as dominant among fours and fives does not, like the emergence of Yin and Yang, spring from the inner necessities of Chinese thought. The appendices of the *Changes* and the Yellow Emperor documents from Mawangdui both ignore them. *Huainanzi* does use them, but not in the cosmogony we examined in Part 3, in which the primary set is still the Four Seasons. But the appeal of the Five Powers to rulers became an irresistible consideration with the unification of the empire and then the final suppression of the fiefs (the Prince of Huainan is the last patron of the old style of philosophy). In 221 BCE the First Emperor, informed of Zou Yan's theory by men from his state of Qi, announced the ascendancy of Water, adopted black as the colour for dress and banners and, assuming further correlations with seasons and numbers, shifted the New Year to the first day of winter and rode a six-foot chariot with six horses.[65] The *fangshi* 方士 "men of secret arts" from Qi and Yan in the North-East who claimed the authority of Zou Yan also interested him in the secrets of immortality. The rapid fall of Qin raised the question whether the reign of Water ended with it, eagerly debated until in 104 BCE the Emperor Wu (武帝) finally recognised the return of Soil. It was the Emperor Wu (140–87 BCE) who took the historic step of taking Confucianism as the state ideology, but he too patronised *fangshi* from the North-East who promised immortality. It is in this atmosphere of competition for favour in the new Imperial courts that Dong Zhongshu 董仲舒 (c. 179–c. 104 BCE) rooted Confucian morality in a cosmology which had originated in the arts of physicians and diviners, by fitting the five cardinal virtues into the system of correspondences.

It is commonly assumed that any systematisation of fours or fives implies the Five Processes in the generation order as prime correlate, an assumption still unshaken in Rickett's recent and important translation of part of *Guanzi*, although he notices that it has been questioned by Toda Toyosaburō.[66] One may offer the general objection, however, that such correlations are more likely to emerge from the problems of organising ritual than from proto-scientific speculation. May we not be insulting the intelligence of Zou Yan and the rest of them if we suppose them to be explaining natural phenomena by correspondences fancied in their own heads rather than rooted in traditional practice? There is more than one indication that on the contrary the Five Processes have been pulled into an already existing system co-ordinating with the pairs East/West and South/North, which in relation to the Emperor facing South become (as in *Heguanzi*[67]) Left/Right and Front/Back. Thus the numbers ascribed to the Five Processes accord with neither the generation nor the conquest cycle, but make sense if the counting is from the ruler's position in the North and at the back.

```
              Front
                2
   Left 3      5      4 Right
                1
              Back
```

A similar point arises with the Five Sounds. As notes in the pentatonic scale their sequence is Gong 宮, Shang 商, Jiao 角, Zhi 徵, Yu 羽, with Gong as fundamental. We do find this sequence observed in the system of *Heguanzi*[68] if we assume that Soil (treated separately at the end) has its standard position between Fire and Metal.

East	South	Centre	West	North
Spring	Summer		Autumn	Winter
Wood	Fire	Soil	Metal	Water
Zhi	Yu	Gong	Shang	Jiao

Here it is plain that the scale with Gong at the centre has been fitted to the seasons and the generation cycle; the fitting to the corresponding directions is merely a consequence of this initial choice. But this is not the order of the *Lüshi chunqiu* system which became standard, nor of the variant with Yu and Zhi reversed which appears in *Guanzi*.[69]

East	South	Centre	West	North
Spring	Summer		Autumn	Winter
Wood	Fire	Soil	Metal	Water
Jiao	Zhi	Gong	Shang	Yu

Why is the sequence of the scale dislocated? Presumably because the *Lüshi chunqiu* and *Guanzi* (unlike *Heguanzi*) refuse to break with a traditional correlation of the sounds with the directions, and must therefore fit them to the counterparts of the directions in the Four Seasons and Five Processes.

	South Zhi or Yu	
East Jiao	Centre Gong	West Shang
	Yu or Zhi North	

This conclusion agrees with Kenneth Robinson's proposal that 'the terms *gong*, *shang*, *jiao*, *zhi* and *yu* originally referred to the positions occupied by certain instruments used in controlling the music and dancing,' and that 'the earliest Chinese conception of a scale was not, as in the West, that of a ladder ascending from low to high or descending from high to low pitch, but of a court in which the notes are arranged on either side of the chief or *gong* note.'[70]

That the *Wu xing* were imposed on an older system of fives co-ordinated with the Six *Qi*, causing some rearrangements, is still visible in the calendar chapters of *Guanzi*. These calendars differ from the one in the *Lüshi chunqiu* in that the *Wu xing* are independent of correlations, or subsidiary, or absent altogether; moreover their five gods are missing, they are explicitly distinguished from *qi*, and there is still correlation of the fives with *qi* among which Yang and Yin are sunshine and shade. They are evidence of the gradual intrusion of the *Wu xing*, starting perhaps from the co-ordination with the cardinal points which we have admitted may well be as old as the cult of the five gods.

(1) *Wu xing* 五行 (ch. 41). This is the only chapter of *Guanzi* which uses the term *Wu xing* (its variants appear nowhere in the book). But there are no correlations at all, even with the seasons; the Five Processes are fitted to 72-day divisions of the 360-day year. The sequence, however, follows not the conquest but the generation order, suggesting co-ordination with at any rate the skeleton figure of the cardinal points round the centre. An exceptional feature of this calendar is that the effects of behaviour inappropriate to the time are mostly specific disasters to the royal family, which points to origin in a divination system.

(2) *Qingzhongji* 輕重己 (ch. 85) This calendar is an arrangement of fours, wholly independent of the *Wu xing*.

A	B	C	D
Spring	Summer	Autumn	Winter
East	(South)	West	North
Green	Yellow	White	Black

Its peculiarity, as Rickett notices,[71] is that summer corresponds to not red but yellow. The simplest explanation is that when red was added to complete the scheme of five it was found more convenient to fit red to Fire and yellow to Soil.

(3) *Si shi* 四時 (ch. 40). Here the prime correlates are the Directions: the *Wu xing* do enter, but as remote subsidiaries, in this formula:

Guanzi 2/78/2
東方曰星，其時曰春，其氣曰風，風生木與骨……此謂星德。

'The East: stars. The season: spring. The *qi*: wind. Wind generates wood and bone…. This one calls the Power of the stars.'

	A	B	Between	C	D
	East	South	Centre	West	North
	Stars	Sun	Soil/Year	*Chen* 辰	Moon
	Spring	Summer	All seasons	Autumn	Winter
(*Qi*)	Wind	Yang	—	Yin	Cold
(Generated)	Wood and bone	Fire and *qi* of body	Skin	Metal and nails	Water and blood

The "Between" position gives trouble as usual. Wood, fire and the rest are explicitly distinguished from *qi*, and although the introduction to this chapter displays a fully dualistic conception of Yin and Yang, within the scheme they are plainly still shade and sunshine, surviving from some variation on the older correlation with the Six *Qi*. The same applies to the next calendar.

(4) *Youguan* and *Youguantu* 幼官圖 (ch. 8, 9). This is the most comprehensive of the *Guanzi* calendars, fitted to a lost diagram of the cardinal points grouped round the centre. Unlike the *Lüshi chunqiu* calendar it starts from the centre, but continues in the same clockwise direction (East South West North). It includes the seasons, colours, tastes, sounds (with Zhi and Yu reversed), numbers, and animals (differently ordered) found in the *Lüshi chunqiu*, but omits the *Wu xing* and has the Directions for prime correlate. Like the *Si shi* it correlates also with a series of *qi*:

Between	A	B	C	D
Harmonious	Dry	Yang	Wet	Yin

Toda has concluded that this calendar is wholly independent of the *Wu xing*. He explains the presence of the numbers on the hypothesis that the numbers of the *Wu xing* were transferred to them from the cardinal points.[72] There is a further slight difficulty, that the colours follow the standard order, not that of the *Qingzhongji*. Whether the *Youguan* is wholly independent like the *Qingzhongji* or slightly influenced like the *Si shi* is a question we may leave open. But its basic design derives from a clockwise reading of the Directions starting from the centre, not from the generation order of the *Wu xing* (which requires the centre in not the first but the third place).

The medical classic *Huangdi neijing* (ch. 5) has a huge system of correlations in which the Five Processes of Earth are still secondary to the *qi* of Heaven. This time they are cold, hot, dry, wet and wind, called the "Five *Qi*." The formula is:

Huangdi neijing SBCK (ch. 5) 2/4B/10–5A/4
南方生熱，熱生火……其在天爲熱，在地爲火。

'The South generates heat, heat generates Fire. … In Heaven it is heat, in Earth it is Fire.'

As in the *Zuozhuan* cosmology, they enter the body as the inclinations, a more varied set but still called *zhi* 志.

Ut sup. 2/3A/9
人有五臟，化五氣以生喜怒悲憂恐。

'Man has the Five Viscera, which transform the Five *Qi* and so generate pleasure in, anger against, sadness, worry and fear.' (The rest of the chapter has *si* 思 "thought" for *bei* 悲 "sadness").

	A	B	*Between*	C	D
(*Qi*)	Wind	Hot	Wet	Dry	Cold
(Processes)	Wood	Fire	Soil	Metal	Water
(Viscera)	Liver	Heart	Spleen	Lungs	Kidneys
(Inclinations)	Pleasure	Anger	Thought	Worry	Fear

These correlations (although including colours, tastes, sounds and many more) do not include the Seasons. But earlier in the chapter there is a quotation (introduced by *Guyue* 故曰 'Therefore it is said...'), correlating with the Seasons but not the Processes, which has a different arrangement:

Ut sup. 2/3B/6–10

A	B	C	D
Spring	Summer	Autumn	Winter
Wind	Hot	Wet	Cold

Ch. 3, which likewise correlates with the Seasons but not the Processes, has the latter arrangement throughout (once with "*qi*" for "wind"). Plainly this is the original system, later adapted to the Five Processes by substituting "dry" for "wet" as more appropriate to Metal and transferring "wet" to Soil. The point is of great interest because we find ourselves with the missing link between the original Six *Qi* and the muddled remains of them adapted to the intrusion of the Five Processes. The old correlation of four of the Six *Qi* (dropping light and dark) with the Four Seasons may be recovered from *Zuozhuan* Zhao 4/1:

……則冬無愆陽，夏無伏陰，春無淒風，秋無苦雨。

'In winter there will be no transgressing *yang* (sunshine, heat) and in summer no lurking *yin* (shade, cold), in spring no chill winds and in autumn no bitter rains.'

The contrast between the undesired pairs suggests that sunshine and shade would be out of season but wind and rain merely excessive for the season, so that the correlations should be:

A	B	C	D
Spring	Summer	Autumn	Winter
Wind	Sunshine	Rain	Shade

The *Huangdi neijing* has simply abstracted from sunshine, rain and shade the properties which distinguish them:

Wind	Hot	Wet	Cold

(Cf. ut sup (ch. 69) 20/3A/7, an account of the Five *Qi* with "rain and wet" for "wet")

Returning to the *Guanzi* calendars, one sees that the *Youguan* has taken a similar course, but retaining sunshine and shade (Yin and Yang) and substituting both members of "dry/wet" for "wind/rain" to make a perfectly symmetrical scheme:[73]

| Dry | Sunshine | Wet | Shade |

The *Si shi* calendar seems to derive from a version in which "cold" has already substituted for "shade" but sunshine remains. This would connect with the five "portents" (*shuzheng* 庶徵), the eighth of the sets in the *Hongfan*, 'rain, sunshine (*yang* 暘), warm, cold, wind' (雨，暘，燠，寒，風), which on the same pattern would correlate as follows with the Seasons:

| Wind | Yang or Warm | Rain | Cold |

The *Si shi* finds it necessary to introduce Yin beside Yang, but refuses to discard the obviously appropriate "cold" for winter:

| Wind | Yang | Yin | Cold |

The translation of *Wu xing* by "Five Phases" becomes appropriate with the full development of a cosmology in which they divide out of the universal *qi*, as in the *Chunqiu fanlu* ascribed to Dong Zhongshu.

Chunqiu fanlu (ch. 59) SBCK 13/7A/5
天地之氣,合而爲一,分爲陰陽,判爲四時,列爲五行。行者行也。其行不同,故謂之五行。

'The *qi* of Heaven and Earth join as the One, divide as Yin and Yang, halve as the Four Seasons, assume an arrangement as the Five Processes. "Process" is proceeding; they proceed dissimilarly, and are therefore called the "Five Processes."'

The *qi* advances, warms and brightens as the Yang, retreats, chills and darkens as the Yin; temporally, the rising Yang divides into the *qi* of spring and summer, the rising Yin into the *qi* of autumn and winter; spatially, they proceed from East (spring) and South (summer) through the centre to West (autumn) and North (winter), condensing to become in turn wood, fire, soil, metal and water. The *Wu xing*, then, are the *qi* proceeding through five phases. They are not, strictly speaking, either the processes themselves or the phases themselves, but in the absence of an exact English equivalent the translation "Five Phases" becomes convenient.

How much of the *Chunqiu fanlu* is authentic is a still open question which we shall pass over. We shall conclude by verifying that the old distinctions between the "materials," their "Powers" and their "Processes" are still maintained in *Huainanzi*. The calendar chapter (ch. 5) follows the *Lüshi chunqiu* in mentioning only their Powers. Ch. 8, after a lengthy account of the misuses of wood, water, soil, metal and fire for articles of luxury by extravagant rulers, concludes:

Huainanzi (ch. 8) Liu 8/14A/9f
夫天地之生財也本不過五。聖人節五行，則治不荒。

'The materials (*cai* 財) generated by Heaven and Earth basically do not exceed five;

when the sage is economical with the Five Processes, government is not wasteful.'

The passage utilised above[74] which reconciles their conquest and generation orders first gives a name to them in identifying the "Between" members of the sets of colours, tastes and "positions" (*wei* 位, the centre and cardinal points).

Huainanzi (ch. 4) Liu 4/11B/1
位有五材，土其主也。

'For the positions there are the Five Materials, of which Soil is the chief.'

This section too concludes with a reference to their Processes, to the ways in which the materials behave when put to use.

Huainanzi (ch. 4) Liu 4/11B/4–6
是故以水和土，以土和火，以火化金，以金治木。木復反土，五行相治，所以成器用。

'For this reason one uses water to soften

soil, soil to calm fire, fire to transform metal, metal to regulate wood; and with wood the cycle returns to soil. The Five Processes regulate each other, as the means of perfecting tools and utensils.'

We conclude with a historical summing-up.

(1) Down to 300 BCE philosophers had only a bare cosmological scheme, the Way, Heaven and Earth, the Four Seasons, the 10,000 things. But outside the philosophical schools, the court astronomers, physicians, musicmasters and diviners had a cosmology in which colours, sounds and tastes correlate with the Six *Qi* of Heaven (which included *yang* "sunshine" and *yin* "shade"), and the Five *Xing* (processes) of Earth give way to each other in the conquest cycle. There was a state cult of the Five Processes, which may already have correlated them with the centre and Four Directions.

(2) After 300 BCE the philosophical schools came to accept the Yin and Yang as the *qi* which are the assimilating and differentiating

influences behind chains of pairs.

(3) Outside the philosophical schools, Zou Yan (c. 250 BCE) explained the rise and fall of dynasties by the conquest cycle of the Powers (*de*) behind the Five Processes, and advised rulers who aspired to found the coming dynasty to correlate their ritual acts with the Power of Water. This required a shift of fours and fives from the Six *Qi* to the Five Powers, with the result that the placing of the Powers in the Four Directions implied motion in a generation cycle corresponding to the Four Seasons.

(4) During the 3rd century BCE cosmology enters philosophical literature in *Guanzi* and the *Lüshi chunqiu*. From the unification in 221 BCE by the First Emperor reigning by the Power of Water, the surviving schools took over the whole system of correspondences now indispensable to influence at court. The Five *Xing* (now translatable as "Five Phases") took next place to Yin and Yang, as the *qi* which assimilate and differentiate chains of fours and fives, and move all of them through the generation and conquest cycles.

FINDING LIST

GJC *Guoxue jiben congshu* 國學基本叢書
HY   Harvard-Yenching sinological index series
SBBY *Sibu bei yao* 四部備要
SBCK *Sibu congkan* 四部叢刊
SKQS *Siku quanshu* 四庫全書

Ch'en Meng-chia 陳夢家, "The origin of Wu-hsing," *Yenching Journal* 24(1938), 35–53.

Chen Qiyou 陳奇猷, *Han Feizi jishi* 韓非子集釋 Beijing 1958.

Cullen, C. "A Chinese Eratosthenes of the flat earth: a study of a fragment in *Huai Nan tzu*," Bulletin of the School of Oriental and African Studies 39/1 (1976), 107–127.

Derrida, Jacques. *Of Grammatology*, translated G.C. Spivak, Baltimore 1976.

Graham, A.C. (1) *Later Mohist logic, ethics and science*, London and Hong Kong, 1978.
(2) *Reason and spontaneity*, London 1985.
(3) *Studies in Chinese philosophy and philosophical*

literature, Singapore 1986.

Granet, Marcel. *La pensée chinoise*, Paris 1950 (1st edition 1934).

Guoyu 國語, Shanghai 1978.

Heguanzi 鶡冠子 *Wanyou wenku* 萬有文庫

Ho Peng Yoke, *Li, Qi and Shu: an introduction to Science and Civilization in China*, Hong Kong 1985.

Huang Hui 黃暉, *Lunheng jiaoshi* 論衡校釋, Taipei 1983.

Jakobson, Roman. *Selected writings* v. 2, The Hague and Paris 1971.

Jingfa 經法 (*Mawangdui Hanmu boshu* 馬王堆漢墓帛書 Beijing 1976).

Kepler, Johannes. *Epitome of Copernican astronomy* Books 4 and 5, translated Charles Glenn Wallis, in *Great books of the world* v. 16, Chicago 1952.

Kuhn, Thomas S. *The structure of scientific revolutions*, Chicago 1970.

Laozi Jiaben juanhou gu yishu 老子甲本卷後古佚書

Lau D.C. *Confucius: the Analects*, Penguin Classic, 1979.

Lévi-Strauss, Claude. *La pensée sauvage*, Paris 1962.

Major, John (1) "A note on the translation of two technical terms in Chinese science," Early China 2 (1976) 1–3.
(2) "The Five Phases, magic squares and schematic cosmography," *Explorations in early Chinese cosmology*, edited Henry Rosemont Jr. *Journal of the American Academy of Religion Studies* 50/2 (1984), 133–166.

Morohashi Tetsuji 諸橋轍次, *Dai Kan-Wa jiten* 大漢和辭典 Tokyo 1955–1960.

Needham, Joseph. *Science and civilisation in China*, Cambridge 1954ff.

Qian Mu 錢穆, *Xian-Qin zhuzi xinian* 先秦諸子繫年, Taipei 1981.

Rickett, W. Allyn. *Guanzi: political, economic and philosophical essays from early China* v. 1, Princeton 1985.

Ryle, Gilbert. *The concept of mind*, London 1949.

Saussure, Ferdinand de. *Course in general linguistics*, translated by Wade Baskin, London 1974.

Shiji 史記, Beijing 1959.

Shima Kunio 島邦男 *Gogyō shisō to Raiki Getsurei no kenkyū* 五行思想と禮記月令の研究, Tokyo 1971.

Sun Yirang 孫詒讓 *Mozi jiangu* 墨子間詁 Beijing 1954.

Sunzi bingfa xinzhu 孫子兵法新注, Beijing 1977.

Toda Toyosaburō 戸田豊三郎, *Gogyō setsu seiritsu no ichikōsatsu* 五行説成位の一考察 *Shinagaku kenkyū* 支那學研究 12 (11955), 38–45.

Xu Fuguan 徐復觀, *Zhongguo renxinglun shi* 中國人性論史 Taipei 1969.

Xu Weiyu 許維遹, *Lüshi chunqiu jishi* 呂氏春秋集釋 Beijing 1955.

Yates, Frances. *Giordano Bruno and the Hermetic tradition*, London 1964.

Zhang Xincheng 張心澂, *Weishu tongkao* 偽書通考 Shanghai 1957.

Zhang Zhenze 張震澤, *Sun bin bingfa jiaoli* 孫臏兵法校理 Beijing 1984.

Zuo Yihuan 左益寰 *Yin-Yang Wuxingjia di xianquzhe Boyangfu* 陰陽五行家的先驅者伯陽父 *Fudan xuebao* 復旦學報1 (1980), 97–100.

NOTES

1 *Analects* 7/17. The reading 亦 of the Lu 魯 text is preferred, for example, by Lau, 88.
2 *Xunzi* HY 1/29f.
3 *Mozi* HY 41/2 *Sunzi bingfa xinzhu* 58, 155. *Han Feizi* (ch. 19), Chen 307.
4 Cf. *Appendix* p. 138 above.
5 The "Art of war" ascribed to Sun Bin not only mentions the Five Phases but extends their conquest cycle to the Five Colours (*Sun Bin bingfa jiaoli*, Zhang 72, 192f). But this text has historical references down to about 300 BCE (ut sup. 123), so that some of it at least is considerably later than Sun Bin (fl. 353 BCE).
6 *Xunzi* HY 17/39.
7 *Mozi* ch. 68, cf. 49 below.
8 *Mozi* HY 47/48–53.
9 Graham (1) 54f. Cf. *Canons* A1, 77, 83, B43.
10 *Huainanzi* (ch. 3) Liu 3/32A/11–33A. Cf. Cullen op. cit. for a translation and detailed analysis.
11 Evidence for dating Zou Yan is abundant but contradictory; I follow the late dating of Qian Mu (Qian

438–441). The crucial evidence, not quite conclusive, is the nearly contemporary reference in *Han Feizi* (ch. 19) Chen 307 to the defeat of Yan in 242 BCE. This does not positively say that Zou Yan was alive in 242 BCE, but couples him with the defeated general Ju Xin 劇辛 as sharing the blame. According to *Zhanguo ce* 戰國策 SBCK 9/17B/3 Yue Hao 樂毅, Zou Yan and Ju Xin were all invited to Yan by King Zhao 昭 (311–279 BCE) before his 28th year; that is acceptable for Yue Hao, chronologically incredible for Ju Xin, therefore useless as evidence for Zou Yan. The only other evidence likely to be earlier than Sima Qian is a fragment ascribed to *Huainanzi* in *Taiping yulan* 太平御覽 SBCK 14/2B/9, according to which there was frost in summer when King Hui 惠 (278–272 BCE) of Yan imprisoned him in spite of his loyal service. Sima Qian records him as visiting the Lord of Pingyuan (平原君, died 252 BCE) later than the relief of Handan 邯鄲 in 257 BCE (*Shiji* ch. 16, 2370/6, cf. 2369); but he not only accepts the historicity of the invitation by King Zhao, he credits Zou Yan with a visit to King Hui 惠 of Liang 梁 (370–319 BCE, cf. ch. 74, 2345), whom he perhaps confused with the King of Yan of the same name.

12 Zou Yan is said to have spoken dismissively of the sophistry of Gongsun Long 公孫龍, but as ambassador from Qi talking with the Lord of Pingyuan, not in debate with the philosopher himself (*Bielu* 別錄 ap. *Shiji jijie* 史記集解 ch. 76, 2370). The listing in *Shiji* (ch. 46) 1895 (cf. also ch. 74, 2346) of Zou Yan

among members of the Jixia 稷下 academy under King Xuan 宣 of Qi (319–301 BCE) is unacceptable if he was still alive in 242 BCE.

13 *Xunzi* HY 6/1–14, 17/51f, 21/21f. *Lüshi chunqiu* ch. 17/7. *Shizi* 尸子 SBBY, A, 14B/3f. *Zhuangzi* ch. 33. *Huainanzi* (ch. 21) Liu 21/8A-9B.

14 *Han Feizi* (ch. 19) Chen 307.

15 *Shiji* (ch. 74) 2344–2348, cf. also (ch. 26) 1259, (ch. 28) 1368f, (ch. 34) 1558, (ch. 44) 1847, (ch. 46) 1895, (ch. 76) 2370.

16 Cf. *Appendix* 153-158ff. above.

17 The calendars at the head of each of ch. 1–12, and the account of the rise and fall of dynasties in ch. 13/2. Xu 13/7A, B.

18 Cf. Huan Kuan *Yantielun* 鹽鐵論 SBCK (ch. 11, 53) 2/14B/4 15A/3. 9/10B–11A. Wang Chong often derides Zou Yan's mythical geography, at most length in *Lunheng* 論衡 SBCK (ch. 31) Huang 477–484. His one item not mentioned by Sima Qian is that according to Zou Yan the Chixian Shenzhou 赤縣神州 in which we are living is the South-Eastern among the nine continents. But Shenzhou is the name of the South-Eastern region of the world in *Huainanzi* (ch. 4) Liu 4/1B/1f; whatever the relation to Zou Yan's system (cf. Major (2)133–145), the knowledge that the Chixian Shenzhou mentioned by Sima Qian would be in the South-East is not necessarily proof of first-hand acquaintance with Zou Yan's writings.

19 The fragments of Zou Yan are translated complete in Needham, v. 2, 236–258. Of these only the six shortest

(Nos 2, 3, 5-8) are attested as quotations from his writings.
20 Jakobson, in particular "Two aspects of language," pp. 239-259.
21 Cf. Graham (3), pp. 7-66.
22 Granet, 82.
23 ut sup. 35.
24 Ryle, 149, 151.
25 *Jingfa* 94f.
26 Kepler, 864.
27 ut sup. 854.
28 ut sup. 855.
29 Kepler, 853.
30 Lévi-Strauss, 57.
31 ut sup. 64.
32 Cf. *Appendix* 153-158ff. above.
33 For 5 as the centre between 1-4 and 6-9 cf. *Shangshu dazhuan* SKQS v. 68/405.
34 *Zuozhuan* Zhao 31/7, Ai 9/4.
35 *Huainanzi* (ch. 4) Liu 4/11A.
36 Major (2), 146-150.
37 Needham, v. 3, 55-62.
38 ut sup. 61.
39 Major (2), 163 n. 17.
40 *Guanzi* GJC 3/119/8, *Huangdi neijing* SBCK 1/11A/9.
41 Graham (2) 1-13, 109-113, 184-192.
42 Cf. Zhuang 22/3. Zhao 5/1, 32/6.
43 Needham, v. 2, 340-345.
44 Six *Qi*: *Zuozhuan* Zhao 1/*fu* 8, 25/2. *Guoyu* (ch. 3) 132.
45 Cf. 110-114 above.

46 *Guanzi* GJC 2/15/1–16/1.
47 *Zhuangzi* HY 1/21, 4/38.
48 ut sup. 2/13, 4/37f. 6/49, 56.
49 *Shiji* (ch. 74) 2344.
50 *Zuozhuan* Zhao 4/1.
51 Cf. Major (1).
52 The *Zuozhuan* mentions the *liu fu* once (Wen 7/*fu*), the *wu cai* twice (Xiang 27/*fu* 2, Zhao 11/4), the *Wu xing* three times (Zhao 25/2, 29/*fu* 4, 32/6). Although we can hardly put much trust in the genuineness of speeches in the *Zuozhuan*, it is of some interest that there is no reference to the *liu fu* or *wu cai* later than 531 BCE (11th year of Duke Zhao), and none to the *Wu xing* earlier than 517 BCE (25th year). All references to the *Wu xing* except the earliest, as well as both the cases of their conquests being used in divination (Zhao 31/7, Ai 9/4), are ascribed to a single man, the Jin 晉 historiographer Mo (吏 墨), speaking between 513 and 484 BCE. In a case where three diviners give answers (Ai 9/4), only Mo appeals to the conquest cycle. There are only two very short speeches of Mo which do not mention the *Wu xing* or the conquests (Zhao 29/*fu* 5, 32/3). Although the reference in 517 BCE is by You Ji 遊吉 of Zheng 鄭, it is in answer to an inquiry by Zhao Jianzi 趙簡子 of Jin, as are all but one of Mo's in the *Zuozhuan* (the exception is Zhao 29/*fu* 4) as well as his answers in the *Guoyu* (ch. 15, 496; 497) and *Lüshi chunqiu* (ch. 20/4, Xu 20/15B). One is tempted to infer that the *xing* as processes were first abstracted

from the materials by diviners in Jin introducing the cycle of the conquests a little before 517 BCE. Unlike the *Wu xing*, the hexagrams appear in speeches dated as early as 674 BCE (Zhuang 22/3), Yin and Yang as early as 644 BCE (Xi 16/1). This difference does not however hold for the *Guoyu*, where the only example of *Wu xing* (ch. 4, 170) is placed in the time of Duke Xi 僖 of Lu (659–627 BCE). The *Guoyu* also contains what have often been taken as the oldest references to the Yin and Yang (by Boyangfu 伯陽父 in 780 BCE, ch. 1, 26) and the *Wu xing* (enumerated, although without a name for the set, by the Historiographer Bo 史伯 answering Duke Huan 桓 of Zheng (806–774 BCE), ch. 16, 515). Zuo Yihuan (op. cit) plausibly identifies the two speakers, and draws the conclusion (accepted by Ho Peng Yoke, 15) that the standard system combining Yin-Yang and *Wu xing* goes back to the end of Western Zhou. That the system specific to the *Zuozhuan* and *Guoyu* was already established by the 8th century BCE is not impossible. But both speeches are suspiciously far-sighted anticipations of the coming fall of Western Zhou, and even if we extend our credulity as far as the beginnings of Eastern Zhou we must surely dismiss them as later diagnoses of the catastrophe. There is another reference widely used in studies of the *Wu xing* which, if accepted, would imply that they were recognised as *qi* long before the 3rd century BCE. Ch'en Meng-chia found it in an inscription of about 400 BCE, on the theme of nurturing the *qi*. This is accepted by Rickett (p. 150 n. 7) and by Needham, who translates the inscription (Needham v. 2, 242):

> 行氣立則畜……
> '(When the) *qi* of the elements (is) settled, condensation (ie. corporeality) (is brought about)…'

But Ch'en Meng-chia himself understood *xing qi* 行氣 as "guide the *qi*." *Xing qi* in this sense (Morohashi 34029/83, 85) is already attested in *Zuozhuan* Zhao 9/*fu* 2 (quoted p. 133 above). His sole evidence for a connection with the *Wu xing* is the graph with the "fire" radical used in the inscription for *qi* (炁), and his own theory that the *Wu xing* originated from the custom of changing fuels through the four seasons, sometimes called *xing huo* 行火 "making fire proceed" (Chen 37, 46f). Even if his whole case were accepted, the inscription would be evidence only for some kind of connection between the custom and the nurture of *qi*, not necessarily through the *Wu xing*.

53 Sima Qian uses only *de* when referring to Zou Yan's doctrine or to the First Emperor's application of it. Cf. *Shiji* (ch. 6) 237/16–238/2 (ch. 26) 1259/12, 14 (ch. 28) 1368/15. One of Zou Yan's books was entitled "Ends and starts of the Five Powers" (五德終始) ut sup. (ch. 28) 1369 n.5. One of the First Emperor's applications of the doctrine was to rename the Yellow River "Water of the Power" (德水, ut sup. (ch. 6) 238/1 (ch. 26) 1259/14). As Nathan Sivin has pointed out to me, the only reference to *Wu xing* by

anyone quoting the writings of Zou Yan is in a note by Pei Yin (ut sup. (ch. 28) 1369 n.11); this may be paraphrase rather than citation, although we cannot be certain that Zou Yan avoided the term in all contexts.

54 The calendar chapters use *de* (ch. 1/2, 4/1, 7/1, 10/1, Xu 1/3A, 4/2B, 7/2A, 10/2A). The account of the conquest cycle of the dynasties uses *qi* (ch. 13/2, Xu 13/7A, 7B).
55 Cf. *Liu tao* 六韜 SBCK 3/16A/10, where the *wu cai* 五材 are courage, wisdom, benevolence, trustworthiness and loyalty.
56 Cf. *Guanzi* GJC (ch. 53) 3/9/6 夏賞五得 'In summer reward the Five Virtues.'
57 Cf. 164ff. above.
58 For the controversy over the date of the *Hongfan* cf. Zhang Xincheng 155–187, passim. Xu Fuguan 537–555. On the present analysis of the historical development we can at least dismiss arguments that it must be later than Zou Yan; its doctrine of the *Wu xing* belongs to the earlier phase represented by the *Zuozhuan*.
59 *Shangshu* 尚書 HY 07/0027, 24/0055.
60 *Huainanzi* (ch. 8) Liu 8/10B–13B.
61 *Zuozhuan* Zhao 29/*fu* 4.
62 *Zuozhuan* Zhao 31/7, Ai 9/4.
63 *Zuozhuan* Zhao 29/*fu* 4.
64 Shima 5.
65 *Shiji* (ch. 6) 237, (ch. 28) 1368.
66 Rickett 166.

67 *Heguanzi* (ch. 6) 27, cf. (ch. 17) 108. Without proposing to date it more exactly, I accept this syncretistic work as belonging, with the *Lüshi chunqiu* and *Huainanzi,* to the last phase of the age of the philosophers. Its language preserves the old distinctions between negative *fu* 弗 (with transitive verb and implied object) and *bu* 不, and between pronouns *wu* 吾 ('I, my') and *wo* 我. The argument at the head of ch. 8 that excessive punishment interferes with the generation of water and the conquest cycle of the Five Phases is surely aimed at Qin. The organisation of the empire in ch. 9 uses the titles of officials specific to Chu. Although ch. 12 is full of parallels with known sources which it may have pillaged, all are of the 2nd century BCE (the 'Owl *fu*' of Jiayi 賈誼, *Zhanguo ce*, the Mawangdui "Yellow Emperor" documents).

68 ut sup. (ch. 10) 70f.

69 Apart from the *Youguan* chapter (cf. p. 156 above), the note Zhi is correlated with the colour black (and therefore with North and winter) in *Guanzi* (ch. 58) 3/21 /7; the colour for Yu is missing.

70 Needham v. 4/1, 159.

71 Rickett 163.

72 Toda 40f.

73 The relation between the *qi* of the *Youguan* and *Zuozhuan* Zhao 4/1 was already noticed by Toda (Toda 41).

74 p. 95 above.

INDEX

abstract knowledge, 9
alchemy, 2, 16, 17
Analects, 18, 20, 132
analytic reason/thinking, 3–4, 6, 12, 13, 17, 32, 33, 43, 61, 67, 71
animals, 28, 39, 52, 57, 64–65, 76, 84, 156
Aristotle/Aristotelian, 12, 15, 53

Baudelaire, Charles, 79
bei 悲 "sadness," 158
benevolence, 19, 116, 138, 178 n. 55; *see also* five kinds of conduct
"Between," 72, 74, 80, 82, 83, 86, 101, 106, 121, 129, 155, 156, 158, 164
bian 辯 "dialectic," 21
Bielu 別錄, 172 n. 12
binary oppositions, 49, 58, 68, 75, 78, 89, 101, 121, 136
birds, 28, 57, 61, 64, 66, 68, 69, 84

black, 20, 24, 33, 36, 76, 79, 81, 82, 83, 84, 86, 88, 92, 93, 106, 116, 147, 149, 154, 179 n. 69
Bo 史伯, historiographer, 176
Book of Changes (*yi* 易), 1, 18, 19, 25, 28, 91, 98, 121–27, 148
Book of Documents, 87, 141, 143
Book of Rites, 84
Boyangfu 伯陽父, 176 n. 52
bu 不, 179 n. 67
building-blocks of thought, 4

cai 才 "the stuff one is made of," 138
cai 材 "materials," 140; *see also wu cai* 五材
calendars, 84, 114, 153, 156, 161, 173 n. 17
calendrical schemes, 24–25, 85, 92, 106
Canons, 18, 21
causal explanation, 14–15, 21, 34, 63, 102
causal thinking, 14, 34, 102

chains of oppositions, 1, 30, 31–32, 40, 43, 80, 148, 166
Changes, see Book of Changes
Chen 辰, 94, 155
Cheng 稱, 49
Chinese ideas, 9–10; *see also* Chinese thought
Chinese philosophy, 9, 28, 34, 119
Chinese thought, 1, 9–10, 43, 75, 126–27, 136, 148
Chixian Shenzhou, 赤縣神州, 173 n. 18
Christianity, 51, 73, 77
Classical Chinese, 5, 45
Confucian cosmology, *see* cosmology, Confucian, 18
Confucianism, 149
Confucius, 10, 12, 17, 18, 24, 149
conjunctions of events, "appropriate" (*yi* 宜), 21: "necessary" (*bi* 必), 21
controlled experiment, 15, 34
correlative ratios, 6
correlative switch, 8
correlative system-building, 2, 3, 16, 61, 80
correlative thinking, in the arts, 79–80 *passim*, 105, 119, 120: general nature of, 1 *passim*, 27
cosmic pairs, 134

cosmological speculation, 1
cosmology, Chinese, 2 *passim*, 25 *passim*: Confucian, 1, 25, 26

Dagong Diao 大公調, 135
Dao 道 "Way," 55, 56, 58, 119, 121, 122, 127, 165
de 德 "Powers," "power, virtue," 84, 137, 138, 166, 177 n. 53, 178 n. 54
Derrida, Jacques, 51
deshui 德水 *see* "Water of the Power"
"Discovery of how to discover," 15, 21, 34
divination, 2, 18, 19, 20, 23, 25, 87, 103, 123, 144, 146, 154, 175 n. 52; *see also Book of Changes*
Dong Zhongshu 董仲舒, 149, 162
Dui 兌 "Marshes" trigram, 124
Duke Huan 桓 of Zheng 鄭, 176
Duke Xi 僖 of Lu 魯, 176
duty, 138

Eight Trigrams, 2, 91, 101, 123–25
"Ends and starts of the Five Powers," *see wu de zhongshi*

esoteric knowledge, 23–24, 149; *see also fangshi*

fangshi 方士 "men of secret arts," 23–24, 25, 149
Faustus, 16
Five Colours, 2, 86, 92, 106, 131, 146, 171 n. 5
Five Creatures, 86
five kinds of conduct, 19, 138
Five Materials, 137, 143, 164
Five Notes, 75, 86
Five Phases, 2, 18, 19, 21, 24, 25, 33, 75 *passim*, 129 *passim*, 171 n. 5, 179 n. 67
five "portents," *shuzheng* 庶徵, 161
Five Powers, *see wu de* 五德
Five Processes, *wu xing* 五行 (*see also* Five Phases); 85, 94, 141, 143, 144, 145, 146, 150, 152, 154, 157, 159, 162, 164, 165, 166
Five Rhythms, 131
Five Smells, 2, 86
Five Sounds, 2, 131, 146, 151
Five Tastes, 2, 75, 86, 131, 145, 146
Five Viscera, *wu zang* 五臟, 110, 158
Four Directions, 2, 51, 86, 88, 89, 92, 106, 124, 165, 166
Four Elements, 2
Four Humours, 2

Four Images, 123, 125
Four Seasons, 2, 35, 52, 53, 55, 86, 88, 89, 92, 106, 109, 121, 122, 124, 130, 131, 135, 136, 145, 148, 159, 162, 165, 166, 177
Fourier, Charles, 43, 105
fours and fives, sets of, 2, 75 *passim*, 136, 147, 148, 166
free will, 9
fu 弗 (with transitive verb and implied object) "negative," 179
fu 府 "storehouses," 140; *see also liu fu*

Gadamer's "fusion of horizons," 10
Galileo, 16, 71
Gen 艮 "Mountains" trigram, 124
geomancy, 2, 17
Gestalt, 3, 60
Golden Rule, 11, 12
Gong 宮, 86, 151, 152, 153
Gongsun Long 公孫龍, 23, 172 n. 12
Grand Historiographer, 107
Granet, Marcel, 2, 17, 42, 43, 45, 46
Great Appendix of the Changes, 98, 123
Greek logic, 6
gu 故 "cause," 21, 63

gu 故, *shi gu* 是故, *shi yi* 是以 "Therefore," 63
Guanzi 管子, 24, 85, 92, 110, 150, 152, 153, 154, 155, 156, 161, 166
Gun 鯀, 143
Guoyu 國語, 19, 130, 143, 175 n. 52, 176
Guyue 故曰 'Therefore it is said…,' 159

Han 漢 dynasty, 25, 26, 28, 46, 85, 136, 140, 145,
Han Fei 韓非, 1, 17, 18
Handan 邯鄲, 172
He 和, physician, 130
Heaven and Earth, 22, 28, 35, 55, 56, 57, 58, 111, 112, 118, 121, 124, 135, 145, 162, 163, 165
Heguanzi 鶡冠子, 152, 179 n. 67
Hermes Trismegistus, 16, 84
Hongfan 洪範 "Grand Scheme," 87, 91, 99, 141, 144, 145, 161, 178 n. 58
Huainanzi 淮南子, 22, 23, 51, 53, 54, 58, 69, 89, 91, 95, 103, 136, 138, 141, 143, 148, 163, 164, 172 n. 11, 173 n. 18, 179 n. 67
Huan Kuan 桓寬 25, 26, 173 n. 18
Huangdi 黃帝, *see* Yellow Emperor
Huangdi neijing 黃帝内經 "Inner classic of the Yellow Emperor," 109, 110, 133, 157, 160
Huangji jingshi shu 皇極經世書, 125
Hui 惠, King, of Liang 梁, 172 n. 11
Hui 惠, King, of Yan 燕, 172 n. 11
Huainan, Prince of, 148
huozheng 火正 "director of fire," 143

Jakobson, Roman, 35, 37, 38, 174 n. 20
Jiao 角, 151, 152, 153
Jie 戒 chapter of *Guanzi*, 134
Jin 晉, 175, 176
Jin 晉, Marquis of, 130
Jin 金 "metal," 64
Jixia 稷下 academy, 173 n. 12
Ju Xin 劇辛, 172

Kabbalah, 16
Kan 坎 "Water" trigram, 124
Kanshi 甘誓, 143
Kant/Kantian, 11, 115
Kepler, Johannes, 16, 51, 52, 53, 72, 73, 79, 83, 102, 127
Kuhn, Thomas, 6, 8, 9; Kuhnian paradigm, 15
Kun 坤 "Earth" trigram, 124

La pensée chinoise, see Granet, Marcel
language, 3–4, 10–11, 29, 40, 45, 104
Laozi 老子, 5, 10, 19, 46, 49, 121, 122, 138
lei 類 "kinds," 67
Leibnitz, 126
Lévi-Strauss, Claude, 70, 83
li 理 "patterns," 118
Li 离 "Fire" trigram, 124
light and dark, 30–31, 36, 64, 81, 82, 132, 134, 136, 140
liu fu 六府 "Six Storehouses," 137, 175 n. 52
liu jia 六家, Six Schools, 22
Liu tao 六韜, 178 n. 55
Lunheng 論衡, 173 n. 18
Luo shu 洛書 "Luo Document," 98
Lüshi chunqiu 呂氏春秋, 1, 21, 24, 84, 85, 86, 88, 106, 108, 122, 135, 137, 138, 146, 148, 152, 153, 156, 163, 166, 179 n. 67

manners, *see* five kinds of conduct
mathematised science, 15, 16, 21, 34, 97, 98, 121
Mawangdui manuscripts, 19, 46, 49, 138, 148, 179 n. 67
Mencius, 17, 19, 24, 44, 134, 138

metaphor, and metonymy, 7, 9, 29, 37, 38, 39, 53, 68, 74, 80, 105, 110
metonymy, 73, 79, 80, 105; *see also* metaphor, and metonymy
Mo 吏墨, historiographer, 175
Mohist, 18, 20, 21, 22, 26
Monthly Orders (*Yueling* 月令), 84
Mozi, 17, 20, 26, 46, 87, 130
mutual translatability, *see* translation/translatability

natural phenomena, 19, 150
neire 內熱 "inward heat," 134
Neo-Confucianism, 28
Neo-Taoism, 28
Newton/Newtonian, 16, 103

occultism, 2, 80, 102
One, the, 122, 162
oppositions, 1 *passim*, 30 *passim*, 40, 43, 49, 50–51, 58, 63 *passim*, 75 *passim*, 121 *passim*, 134, 136, 148; *see also* proportional oppositions
'Owl *fu*' of Jiayi 賈宜, 179 n. 67

paradigmatic relations, 30, 35, 36, 38, 42, 53, 60, 67, 115; *see also* syntagmatic relations

parallelism, 5, 40, 45, 46, 47, 48, 49, 58, 59, 60, 68, 69, 70, 97
Pavlov's dog, 39, 79, 103
Pei Yin 裴駰 of the Liu Song 劉宋 dynasty, 139, 178 n. 53
pentatonic scale, 88, 151
philosophy, Chinese, 1, 9, 17, 18, 22–23, 28, 34, 119, 123, 148, 165, 166
Pingyuan 平原君, Lord of, 172 n. 11, 12
pre-Han dynasty 22, 23, 46, 137
"Primal Beginning," 55, 63
proportional oppositions, 13, 31, 35, 36, 37, 40, 42, 43, 53, 89, 116
proto-sciences, 2, 12, 15, 17, 19, 21, 22, 32, 70, 93, 96, 102, 103, 150
Pythagorean numerology, 2, 16

qi 氣, 52, 55 passim, 63, 64, 66, 69, 107 passim, 129, 132 passim, 140, 141, 144, 146 passim, 153, 155 passim, 160, 162, 163, 165, 166, 176–77 n. 52, 179 n. 73; see also Six Qi of Heaven,
Qi 齊, State of, 23, 149
Qian 乾 "Heaven" trigram, 124
Qin 秦, King of, 24, 139, 149

qing 清 "clear," 58, 136
Qingzhongji 輕重己, 154, 157
red, 76, 77, 79, 82, 84, 86, 93, 106, 147, 155
right, see five kinds of conduct
Rimbaud, 70–80
Ryle, Gilbert, 6, 7, 8, 9, 44, 46, 48

sagehood, see five kinds of conduct
Saussure's linguistics, 29
schemes of correspondences, 18, 24, 28, 62, 83, 136, 149
science, modern, 14, 16, 34, 43, 72, 103–104, 115: post-Galilean, 15, 16, 62, 74, 103, 114, 119
Scientific Revolution, 6, 8, 13, 35
sets of fours and fives, see fours and fives, sets of,
sha ren 殺人 "killing people," "murder, massacre," 46, 48
shade, 130, 131, 132, 134, 136, 140, 153, 156, 160, 161, 165
Shang 商 dynasty, 147
shang 上 xia 下 "superior/inferior," 73
Shang 商, note of the pentatonic scale, 86, 151, 152, 153
Shangshu dazhuan 尚書大傳, 145

Shao Yong 邵雍, 125
shi 事 "thing to do," 142
Shiji 史記, 24, 27, 172 n. 12
Shizi 尸子, 23
shuizheng 水正 "the director of water," 143
Shuo gua 說卦 "Explanation of the Trigrams," 124
si 思 "thought," 158
Si shi 四時, 155, 156, 157, 161
Sima Qian 司馬遷, 24, 25, 27, 135, 137, 139, 172 n. 11, 173 n. 18, 177 n. 53
Sima Tan 司馬談, 22
Six Diseases, 131
Six Inclinations, 133–34
Six Qi 六氣 of Heaven, 130 *passim*, 145, 146, 153, 156, 159, 165, 166
Sixty-four Hexagrams, 2
solstice, 57, 107, 112
Song 宋 dynasty, 98
square *zhu* 方諸, 59, 66, 67
structuralist approach, 29 *passim*
sun, 16, 26, 30, 31, 32, 36, 53, 56, 57, 58, 60, 62, 63, 65, 66, 67, 72, 81, 82, 90, 94, 155
sun and moon, 52, 56, 59, 64, 65, 66
Sun Bin 孫臏, 171 n. 5
sunshine and shade, 92, 130, 131, 132, 134, 136, 140, 160, 161, 165

Sunzi 孫子, 18
suppression of the classics, 25
Supreme One/Supreme Pole, 122, 123
Symbolist movement, 80
syntagmatic connections, 31, 36, 42
syntagmatic relations, 34, 35, 60, 67, 115
system-building, 2, 3, 16, 61, 80

Taiping yulan 太平御覽, 172 n. 11
Taoist, 5, 26, 134; *see also* Dao 道 "Way"
Three Chen 三辰 (sun, moon, stars), 94
Toda Toyosaburō, 150, 157, 179 n. 73
Transcendental magic of Éliphas Lévi, 103
translation/translatability 10–11
Two Exemplars, 122, 123, 125

Wang Chong 王充, 25, 26, 173 n. 18
"Water of the Power," *deshui* 德水, 177 n. 53
wei 位 "positions," 164
wei 爲 "be, become," 70
Western thought, 9, 11, 13, 21, 32, 43, 44, 77, 79, 116

wisdom, *see* five kinds of conduct
Wittgensteinian "family resemblance," 62
wu 吾 and *wo* 我 pronouns ("I, my"), 179 n. 67
wu cai 五材 "Five Materials," 137, 175 n. 52
wu cai 五材 "Five Talents," 178 n. 55
wu de 五德 "Five Powers," 84–85, 86, 89, 91, 92, 93, 97, 99, 100, 106, 137, 139, 147, 148, 166
wu de 五得 "Five Virtues," 137, 178 n. 56
wu de zhongshi 五德終始 "Ends and starts of the Five Powers," 139, 177 n. 53
Wudi 武帝 Emperor Wu, 149
Wu fang 五方 "Five Directions," 88
Wu xing 五行, *see* "Five Elements," "Five Phases," "Five Processes," and "five kinds of conduct"
Wu xing 五行 chapter of *Guanzi*, 154 *passim*

Xia 夏 dynasty, 147
Xiantian 先天 "Ahead of Heaven" order, 125, 126

Xiaoqu 小取 chapter of *Mozi*, 146
xin 心 "heart," 134
xing 行 "conduct," 138
xing 行 "going," 140, 177
xing huo 行火 "making fire proceed," 177
xing qi 行氣 "guide the *qi*," 177
Xu Fuguan 徐復觀, 130, 140, 143, 178 n. 58
Xuan 宣, King, of Qi, 173 n. 12
xueqi 血氣 "blood and *qi*," 132
Xun 巽 "Wind" trigram, 124
Xunzi 荀子, 18, 20
Xunzi 荀子, 23, 136, 138

Yan 燕, 23, 172 n. 11
yang 暘 "sunshine," 130, 131, 132, 134, 136, 140, 153, 156, 160, 161, 165
Yang Zhu 揚朱, 23
yangsheng 養生 "nurture of life," 134
Yantielun 鹽鐵論, 173 n. 18
Yellow Emperor (Huangdi 黃帝), 27, 109, 146–47, 148, 179 n. 67
Yellow River, 177 n. 53
yi 亦 "also, after all," 18
yi 易 "Changes," see *Book of Changes*
yin 陰 "shade," 130, 131, 132, 134, 136, 140, 153, 156, 160, 161, 165

Yin-Yang 陰陽, 3, 45 *passim*, 129 *passim*
Yin-Yang thinking, 6 *passim*, 43 *passim*
yinyang xiaoxi 陰陽消息 "the growth and diminution of Yin and Yang," 135
yinyang zhi huan 陰陽之患 "a yin-yang affliction," 134
yongqi 勇氣 "martial spirit," 132
You Ji 遊吉 of Zheng 鄭, 175 n. 52
Youguan 幼官 and Youguantu 幼官圖, 156, 157, 161, 179 n. 73
Youhu clan 有扈氏, 143
Yu 羽, 86, 151, 152, 153, 156, 179 n. 69
yue 曰 particle, 142
Yue Hao 樂毅, 172 n. 11

Zhanguo ce 戰國策, 172 n. 11, 179 n. 67
Zhao 昭, King, 172 n. 11
Zhao Jianzi 趙簡子 of Jin 晉, 175 n. 52

Zhen 震 "Thunder" trigram, 124
zhi 志 "intent, inclination," 115, 133, 158
Zhi 徵, 86, 151, 152, 153, 156, 179 n. 69
Zhou 周 dynasty, 18, 139, 147, 176
zhu, square, *see* square *zhu*
zhu 主 "ruler," 62
Zhuangzi 莊子, 17
Zhuangzi 莊子, 23, 134, 135, 136
zhuo 濁 "muddy," 58, 136
Zisi 子思, 19
zong 宗 "ancestor," 62
Zou Yan 鄒衍, 23 *passim*, 84, 85, 105, 135, 137, 139, 140, 146, 149, 150, 166, 171 n.11, 172 n. 11–12
Zouzi zhongshi 鄒子終始, 26
Zouzi 鄒子, 26
Zuozhuan 左傳, 19, 23, 24, 93, 94, 124, 130 *passim*, 141, 143, 144, 145, 158, 159, 175–77 n. 52, 178 n. 58, 179 n. 73

www.ingramcontent.com/pod-product-compliance
Lightning Source LLC
Chambersburg PA
CBHW020948230426
43666CB00005B/219